P9-CRE-020

TEENS
AT
WAR

TEN TRUE TALES

TEENS ★AT★ WAR

ALLAN ZULLO

SCHOLASTIC INC.

NEW YORK   TORONTO   LONDON   AUCKLAND   SYDNEY
MEXICO CITY   NEW DELHI   HONG KONG   BUENOS AIRES

To Tim Gorospe, with hopes that the only battles he ever faces
are those on the volleyball court. —A.Z.

No part of this publication may be reproduced, stored in a retrieval system, or transmitted in any form or by any means, electronic, mechanical, photocopying, recording, or otherwise, without written permission of the publisher. For information regarding permission, write to Scholastic Inc., Attention: Permissions Department, 557 Broadway, New York, NY 10012.

ISBN-13: 978-0-545-05807-0
ISBN-10: 0-545-05807-4

Copyright © 2008 by The Wordsellers, Inc.

All rights reserved. Published by Scholastic Inc. SCHOLASTIC and associated logos are trademarks and/or registered trademarks of Scholastic Inc.

Lexile is a registered trademark of MetaMetrics, Inc.

12 11 10 9 8 7 6 5 4 3 2   8 9 10 11 12 13/0

Printed in the U.S.A.
First Scholastic printing, September 2008

CONTENTS

TEENS AT WAR

UNDERAGE WARRIORS

★

Throughout history, people from all walks of life have answered the call to duty in times of war. Courageous men and women quit their jobs and left their families to fight for their country's freedom. But adults weren't the only ones willing to sacrifice themselves to defend this country or the ideals upon which it stands.

Teenagers have fought, too, including many who were underage.

Ever since the American Revolution, teenagers have risked their lives to serve in every war this country has fought. Most were motivated by patriotism. Others yearned for travel and adventure. Some ran away from strict parents and broken homes or escaped dead-end lives on the street. Many had visions of returning home after the war as heroes. They were soldiers but still just kids.

The minimum age to enlist in most wars was 16 or 17 — and then only with parental consent. But in reality, much younger teenagers hoodwinked their way into military service by lying about their age, forging papers, and doctoring their birth certificates. Because many recruiters were desperate to sign up anyone who looked old enough, they often turned a blind eye to the teen's youthful appearance or chose not to challenge his lies or enlistment papers.

In addition to the dangers of war, underage teens risked being caught in their dishonesty. Depending on how young they were when their superiors discovered the truth, most underage soldiers were kicked out of the military and sent home or dishonorably discharged for enlisting under false pretenses. The unluckiest ones were tossed in jail. Yes, technically they broke the law, but they did it to serve their country. To them, their "illegal" service was a badge of honor.

Although the Continental army — the regular Patriot force in the Revolutionary War — did not knowingly draft anyone under 16, it had no legal minimum age for service for those who wanted to enlist. As a result, tens of thousands of kids took up arms against the British.

Many more teenagers fought — and died — during the Civil War. Historians estimate that between 150,000 to 250,000 teenage soldiers faced combat in the armies of the Union and Confederacy between 1861 and 1865.

In both these wars, countless boys as young as 10 served as drummers. They not only provided music but also performed an important role in battlefield communications by various rolls and drumbeats that signaled different commands. Although these boys weren't supposed to engage in combat, oftentimes they did.

During World War I, thousands of underage American soldiers fought in Europe. As many as 250,000 boys younger than 16 lied about their age to enlist in the British military to fill the gaps in the ranks left by mounting casualties. Sadly, nearly half of them never came home.

Of the American soldiers who saw combat in World War II and the Korean War, an estimated 200,000 were teenagers who fooled the military and joined before they were of legal age to enlist.

In warfare, most underage soldiers showed their zealous spirit and raw courage, but few were properly prepared for the horrors they would experience. Death, destruction, and disorder were constant companions on the battlefield. For those who didn't lose their lives or limbs, they still lost things dear to them — their childhood and their innocence.

You are about to read 10 gripping, true stories about these warriors. Among them are a 12-year-old sailor who, despite his own injury, helped rescue fellow seamen when their battleship was attacked in World War II . . . a 15-year-old soldier who, in the Korean War, took over command of his squad after their leader was killed . . . the teenage cadets who fearlessly rushed into battle and saved the day during the Civil War . . . and a Revolutionary War hero who, from the age of 15 on, single-handedly and repeatedly proved his strength and valor.

Their accounts are based on memoirs, news reports, oral histories, battle reports, and military files. Using real names, dates, and places, the stories are written as factual versions of their bravery, although certain scenes have been dramatized and some dialogue has been re-created. For realism, the dialogue contains some language and a few words referring to enemy soldiers that by today's standards are considered offensive but were commonly used in the heat of combat back then.

These underage warriors stared the enemy and death in the face and still performed gallantly. They fought as heroes despite their fears — and despite their age.

THE GIANT OF VIRGINIA

PETER FRANCISCO

Peter Francisco stood outside Saint John's Church in Richmond where a tense, important meeting of the Virginia Convention was under way on a cool spring day in 1775. Inside, more than 120 representatives of the British colony — including Thomas Jefferson, George Washington, and Peter's guardian, Judge Anthony Winston — quarreled loudly.

The tall, muscular 14-year-old listened intently through an open window as debate raged over whether Virginia should form a militia to resist the British government's crackdown on civil rights. Peter sensed that a slim majority of representatives were Loyalists and Tories who supported King George III of England. But then Judge Winston's nephew, a fiery lawyer named Patrick Henry, gave an impassioned plea to take military action against the British government, which had sent troops to America to thwart any uprising among the colonists.

Stirred by Henry's call to action, the delegates jumped to their feet and, in a rousing ovation, shouted, "To arms! To arms!" Outside, Peter was moved, too, by the speech and threw his fists in the air, yelling, "To arms! To arms!"

Later that evening over dinner at a tavern, Peter told the judge, "Sir, I want to join the militia. I want to fight for my country."

Judge Winston smiled and said, "That's a worthy and patriotic ambition, and I'm proud you feel that way. But, Peter, you're only fourteen."

"I'm big and strong. Do you know anyone bigger than me?" He had a point. While the average man stood about five feet ten inches, Peter was huge — six feet four inches tall, and he weighed nearly 260 pounds.

"You're simply too young," the judge declared. "Wait a year, and then we'll see."

Just then two men in a hot debate over the colonies' push for independence started throwing punches. "You're a traitor!" snarled one. "You're a gutless coward, afraid to stand up for our rights!" retorted the other. As their fists flew, they jostled the table where Peter and the judge were sitting and knocked over the judge's drink.

"That's enough!" snapped Peter. He rose and, with his left hand, grabbed one of the fighters by the collar and then, with his right hand, seized the other man. To everyone's amazement, the giant teen lifted the combatants into the air and banged their heads together. "If you want to fight, take it outside," he ordered. Then he tossed them out the door to cheers from the patrons.

"Well done, Peter." Judge Winston beamed. "If we go to war, we're certainly going to need strong lads like you."

Peter, an abandoned child, was raised as an indentured servant on Judge Winston's 3,600-acre plantation. Although treated well, he wasn't given a formal education. Peter was an obedient, bright, hard worker who developed muscles of steel while toiling in the fields and in the blacksmith shop. He grew big and fast, and by 13 he towered over the townspeople. They marveled at the strength of the muscular, shaggy-haired teenager. Once, after seeing two calves trapped in a muddy bog, he slogged in and carried them out, one under each arm.

When Peter turned 15, the judge let him enlist as a private in the Tenth Virginia Regiment, which was eventually assigned to General George Washington's Continental army. Months of training proved that even though he was young, Peter was among the strongest. What his fellow soldiers wondered was whether he would be among the bravest. Peter had no doubt when he faced his first battle.

After a grueling all-day hike, 3,500 Continental soldiers camped near Brandywine Creek, southwest of Philadelphia, which at the time was the capital of the young American nation. Washington had spread his forces along fields that bordered the creek, hoping to prevent British General William Howe's 12,500-man force from capturing the city.

Peter and his comrades prepared for battle on the foggy morning of September 11, 1777. "We ain't goin' to let them Redcoats get our capital, right, boy?" George McEvoy, a grizzled Virginian said to Peter. They were crouched behind a stone wall along the crest of a hill of a plowed farmer's field, waiting for the enemy.

"They won't get by me," Peter boasted, clutching his musket. "I don't care if there are more of them than us."

Soon, through the mist, Peter saw the Redcoats emerge from the woods. His heart racing, he watched in awed silence as British artillery launched a covering barrage over the Redcoats' heads and toward the Patriots' line. When the British soldiers drew closer, the Continental soldiers received the order they had been waiting for: "Fire!"

Peter began shooting at the crimson-clad foes. Within seconds, he was engulfed in a world of bloody, smoky madness. The booming thunder of artillery and muskets shook the valley. Cannonballs plowed up the ground. Shelled trees and limbs cracked over his head, and leaves fell by the millions from flying grapeshot. Above the deafening roar, he heard constant orders, "To the right! To the left! Halt! Charge!"

The Patriots' fire swelled to an ear-shattering racket. Despite being peppered with volleys of grapeshot and cannonballs, the Redcoats advanced rapidly and crossed the Brandywine. Before long, the outmanned Continental soldiers broke ranks and retreated.

Peter's regiment and a few other units guarded the rear so the rest of the force could withdraw. Taking up positions in a narrow valley called Sandy Hollow Gap, Peter and the valiant rearguard units held off the British, who up until then had been pursuing the beaten Patriots without encountering much resistance.

But then Peter's musket malfunctioned, so he ran out into the open to recover the weapon of a dead comrade. Because of his enormous size, Peter made an easy target. He felt a sharp pain in his left leg and crumpled to the ground. "I've been shot!" he moaned. More angry than hurt, he got up and limped back behind the wall and started shooting.

"Are you hurt bad?" asked McEvoy.

"I'll be all right," grimaced Peter, trying to ignore the blood that was turning his pants red.

The gutsy Tenth Virginia stalled the British advance for a crucial 45 minutes — just barely enough time for the Continental force to escape, thus preventing an all-out rout. The men of the rear guard then began a slow, orderly withdrawal. During their retreat, Peter winced as he saw the dead and dying, and bodies crushed beneath fleeing wagons. Then he collapsed from loss of blood.

Later, at a makeshift hospital north of Philadelphia, Peter had a musketball removed from his leg. "We lost the battle, didn't we?" grumbled Peter when McEvoy came to visit him.

"Depends how you look at it," McEvoy said. "I heard each side lost about a thousand men. Yes, we were defeated, but it isn't a total loss. In a sense, the Redcoats failed, too, because the Continental army still exists and the rebellion still lives. We'll be back to fight them another day."

"And another day and another day," vowed Peter, perking up.

His wound healing quickly, he rejoined his regiment just in time to fight in the Battle of Germantown on October 4. There, the Continental army tried vainly to hold the forts that protected the lower Delaware River. But a British counterattack forced another Patriot retreat. Peter was disappointed but not discouraged.

However, his life as a soldier took a turn for the worse when he and 450 men were under siege from mid-October to mid-November at Fort Mifflin on Mud Island on the Delaware River. Day after rainy day, British ships bombarded the fort. Peter watched enemy shells fall in the thick mud and sink so low that their blast could not be heard, although he could feel the earth shake. At other times, when the shells burst near the surface, the blasts threw mud 50 feet in the air.

The British also fired grapeshot from their mortars, pelting the Patriots like hail. But Peter and his fellow soldiers collected the grapeshot, loaded it in one of their big guns, and sent it back to its former owners. The brazen teen sometimes caught falling shot in his massive hands before it hit the ground.

The mud and the constant bombardment made it nearly impossible to lie down and get any rest or sleep. Peter thought about sleeping in the barracks. But he changed his mind after several exhausted soldiers flopped into the barracks for a nap and perished — victims of a direct hit.

For four terrible weeks, Peter and his comrades suffered hunger, cold, and fatigue. He never lay down to sleep. He caught catnaps by leaning against the side of a wall.

On November 14, five British ships shelled the fort in a furious attempt to destroy it once and for all. The carnage mounted by the hour. Peter saw five soldiers who were manning one gun get blown up from a perfectly aimed artillery shell.

"We're getting cut down like cornstalks!" shouted McEvoy.

"We need someone to signal our galleys [Continental ships farther up river] to come to our aid," yelled an officer.

Peter grabbed the signal flags, but McEvoy took them from him, saying, "I'm looking for a promotion. Let me do it." The teenager agreed.

McEvoy ran up to the highest point of the fort, attached the flags to a rope, and sent them up the pole. As he headed back, he smiled at Peter who then watched in horror as the Virginian was blown apart by an exploding artillery shell.

Peter kneeled to the ground and wept. But the intense battle made him focus on his own survival. By midday, nearly every cannon in the fort was destroyed. At nightfall, the survivors prepared to escape to the New Jersey shore.

Peter remained with 80 men who, following orders, burned all that was left so the enemy couldn't use it. Then they scurried down to the wharf and hopped into three longboats. However, huge flames from the blazing fort threw enough light that the fleeing Patriots were easily spotted by the British, who began shooting at them.

During the desperate crossing, one of the boats was struck by a cannonball and began to sink. The other two boats came to its rescue under intense shelling. Using his incredible strength, Peter held on to the crippled craft and kept it from sinking while the soldiers scrambled aboard the remaining two boats. The men eventually landed after midnight on the Jersey shore and marched into the pinewoods where their comrades had built welcoming campfires. Peter wrapped himself in his blanket, lay down upon the leaves, and had his first good sleep in a month. He was one of only 250 soldiers who had survived the siege of Fort Mifflin.

A month later, the battle-tested teen joined nearly 12,000 other troops at Valley Forge about 25 miles west of Philadelphia to wait out the winter. Each member of the ragtag army of men, boys, and even grandfathers brought with them his meager possessions — a musket, cartridge box, haversack (knapsack), blanket, plate, and spoon. The lucky ones like Peter had an extra pair of clothes. But others were shirtless and even shoeless.

Under a light snow, the men built 12-man huts for shelter against the winter weather. But, Peter, like thousands of his fellow soldiers, was growing weaker because food and water were scarce. The men sometimes went days without eating.

"Our prospects are indeed dreary," a teenage corporal told Peter. "I thought I had experienced hardships of military life over the past year, but this is appalling. We are now in danger of dying. Ironic, isn't it, in the midst of a plentiful country."

"We must stay determined," said Peter. "If we give up, all is lost. Then our country will never be free."

Although his resolve was strong, his body no longer was. Exposure from the bitter cold, lack of proper nutrition, the inability to keep clean, and living in close quarters with sick soldiers took their toll on Peter. He suffered from high fevers and dysentery, ending up bedridden in a field hospital for two months. He felt fortunate because he survived while more than 2,500 troops died during the cruel winter.

By spring, when food was more abundant and the weather had improved, the teen had regained his health. "Your tour of duty has expired, lad," a lieutenant told him. "You can go home now."

"But our war with the British isn't over," said Peter. "I intend to stay and fight for as long as it takes until we're free." So he reenlisted.

Despite the insufferable hardships the men at Valley Forge had endured, most of the soldiers stuck together, drilled regularly, and were ready to clash again with the British. On June 28, 1778, the Patriots tried to head off the British near Monmouth Courthouse in New Jersey. Under extremely hot, humid conditions, a fierce bloody battle broke out. Once again, Peter was shot, this time in the right thigh. But he kept fighting until a violent evening thunderstorm ended the combat. Although he had sustained a painful wound, Peter recovered and soon returned to the front lines.

In skirmishes big and small, he fearlessly charged into the fray, expertly wielding his sword and firing his weapon. His brute strength and intense spirit bolstered his comrades, who now considered him their best fighter.

One day in July 1779, Peter and his fellow soldiers trekked 14 miles north of New York City for a surprise attack against a vital British fortress at Stony Point, New York. The stronghold, which housed the administrative and command posts of the British forces, was protected by the war's most powerful cannons. Seemingly impenetrable, it stood on a 150-foot-high promontory (a rock outcropping) bordered on two sides by the Hudson River and another side by a swamp. The area on the rock was scraped of all trees, and the fort was ringed by abatises (barricades of downed trees) with sharp branches pointing outward.

Moving quietly in single file, more than 1,100 Continental soldiers reached a clearing about a mile and a half west of Stony Point at about 8 P.M. "I need volunteers for a dangerous but crucial mission," announced Lieutenant Colonel François de Fleury, a French officer who fought with the Patriots.

Without hesitating, Peter stepped forward, and others followed. The teen was placed in one of two 20-man commando units for a hazardous undertaking known in the military as "forlorn hope" because the chances of survival were slim to none.

"In the dead of night, you will carry axes as well as guns and scramble silently up the cliff — a unit on each side — and open gaps in the abatises for our light infantry," De Fleury explained to the brave volunteers. "Then you will move forward and attack the enemy. The rest of the troops will follow behind you. They will march with bayoneted weapons, utter no word, and make no attempt at retreat under pain of death. To aid in the difficult task of identifying friend from foe in the darkness, you will stick a square piece of white paper to the front of your caps."

In the few hours remaining before the deadly mission, the men prepared themselves for combat. Some wrote their wills or what they thought would be their final letters home. Others prayed. Peter visualized bursting into the fort and capturing the flag.

At 11:30 P.M., when most of the British soldiers were asleep, Peter and his fellow commandoes crept up the north and south sides of the promontory in perfect silence while the rest of the Continental force followed. Orders were given in whispers and everyone tread lightly. The quiet only made Peter think more about the dangers he was about to face. Suddenly, a sentry's musket blast broke the stillness, followed by a salvo of gunfire. "We've been discovered!" a soldier shouted.

Peter continued climbing amid the rush of confusion, commands, and clamor of battle. Through the withering barrage of musketballs from the ramparts, Peter scaled the rock. Above him, he heard wild shouts of alarm from the enemy; below him, the shrieks of fallen comrades.

When he reached the first abatis, he chopped his way through it. Then he did the same at the second one, carving a path for the others behind him. Forlorn-hope volunteers were dropping left and right from the defensive barrage. But Peter kept swinging his ax with one hand and holding on to his bayoneted musket with the other.

As one of the first to reach the fort, Peter came face to face with three British soldiers. He threw his ax at the closest one, slaying him instantly. Then Peter grabbed the second soldier's weapon by the barrel and, with his astonishing strength, shoved the butt into the man's face, killing him, too. But at the same moment, the third soldier swept his bayonet at the teen, slicing a nine-inch gash across his stomach.

Peter gasped and cried out in pain. Rather than disable him, the wound enraged Peter. He ignored the bleeding slash and leaped on the third soldier, disarming him before strangling him. Clutching his stomach, Peter staggered to his feet and lurched toward the flagpole, fending off one British soldier after another. When he reached the pole, he grabbed the rope and lowered the British flag. He yanked it off the rope and cried out, "The fort is ours!"

He slumped to the ground in front of the pole, the flag tucked around his wound. He saw his fellow invaders pour into the fort and rout the British in vicious hand-to-hand combat until the foes cried out, "Mercy on us!" and surrendered. Peter heard his triumphant comrades chant, "The fort is ours! The fort is ours!" He felt the ground shake from the captured cannons that the Patriots were now firing on British ships anchored in the river below. And then he passed out.

When Peter regained consciousness in the morning, he noticed his wound was bandaged. "Here," said a young doctor's assistant, handing him the bloodstained British flag. "We found this wrapped around you."

Wincing in pain, Peter sat up and took the flag. He shuffled over to De Fleury and said, "Sir, this is for you. The fort is ours."

"Well done, young man, well done!" beamed the Frenchman. "With a few more big, strong soldiers like you, this war will be over soon."

It was the last major battle of the Revolutionary War in the north. Of the 20 members of Peter's commando unit, 17 were killed or wounded. They were among 63 Patriots killed and 40 wounded. The British suffered 20 deaths and 74 wounded. Another 543 were taken prisoner.

When Peter recovered, he reenlisted in Colonel William Mayo's Virginia Militia Regiment, which joined forces with other militias at Camden, South Carolina, where the British launched a devastating attack.

At dawn on a steamy August day, the Redcoats fired volleys and charged with bayonets. Hundreds of Patriots who had never seen action before panicked, tossing away their muskets and running for their lives.

Seeing the disorderly retreat, Peter stood up and yelled to the fleeing militiamen, "Stop! Stop! Don't run! We must fight! We can lick 'em! Get back here!" But the green troops refused to listen. Now badly outnumbered, the veteran soldiers withdrew into the pine forest and were soon overrun by the enemy.

As Peter headed into the woods, he spotted a British grenadier raising his musket to bayonet Colonel Mayo, who had tripped and fallen. Peter shot the Redcoat just in time. Moments later, a British cavalryman on his horse charged the two men. "Run, Colonel," said Peter. "I'll take care of him."

The colonel sprinted off to round up his men while Peter stood his ground. The cavalryman raised his sword and ordered, "Throw down your musket!"

"I will not!" Peter replied.

The horseman wheeled around to strike him with his sword, but Peter sidestepped him, then swiftly bayoneted the trooper, toppling him from his saddle. Mounting the horse, Peter pretended to be a Tory and yelled to a platoon of Redcoats who had arrived at the scene, "Huzzah, my lads! Let's go after the rebels!"

As he rode ahead, he came across Colonel Mayo who had been captured by two Redcoats. Peter pulled out his sword and killed the pair. He hopped off the horse, handed the reins to the colonel, and urged, "You need to get out of here fast."

"What about you?"

"I can take care of myself, sir."

After the colonel departed, Peter noticed that the retreating Patriots had left behind a cannon on a gun carriage attached to a dead artillery horse. Unwilling to let the British capture the weapon, he ran over and unfastened it. Grunting and grimacing, he lifted the 1,100-pound cannon onto his shoulder and staggered with it back to a group of Continental soldiers who hid it.

Exhausted from this rescue, Peter plopped under a tree. He had barely regained his breath when a British cavalryman burst through the pines. His horse rearing above the teenage soldier, the enemy trooper raised his sword and snarled, "Surrender or die!"

"I give up," Peter said meekly. "My musket is unloaded." Holding the gun barrel, he presented the weapon to the foe. As his would-be captor reached for the musket, Peter flipped it over and thrust its bayonet into the soldier's stomach. Shoving the dying man off the saddle, Peter jumped on the horse and galloped off.

He immediately came across a dozen enemy soldiers. Once again, he rose in the stirrups and pretended to be a Tory, yelling, "Huzzah, my brave boys! We've conquered the rebels!" For the second time that day, Peter pulled off a ruse that allowed him to ride through enemy lines.

Stories of Peter's exploits spread throughout the Continental army, and he became known as the Giant of Virginia and the Hercules of the Revolution.

When George Washington learned that Peter complained his sword was too small, the general ordered the army to forge an especially long weapon for the hulking young soldier. Soon Peter was presented with a unique six-foot broadsword with a sharp five-foot blade — one that he used until the Patriots defeated the British.

"Without him, we would have lost two crucial battles, perhaps the war, and with it our freedom," Washington once said.

After the war, Peter returned to Virginia and went to school where he discovered a love for reading and eventually had his own library. He became a prosperous landowner, was married three times (having been widowed twice), and raised six children. He gained a reputation as a quiet-spoken, kindhearted giant who shelled corn for the poor and took food to old servants. He died in 1831 at age 70 and was buried with military honors in Richmond.

THE SOLDIER WHO WOULDN'T KILL

BENJAMIN B. LEVY

Benjamin Levy and his family sat around the kitchen table in their small New York City home talking about the meaning of the Torah, the five books of the Hebrew Scriptures. As was customary, Ben, 16, his brother Robert, 14, and their parents were staying up all night in honor of the Jewish holiday of Shevuoth, a time when Jews celebrate the Torah and the Ten Commandments.

Ben was conflicted. He believed strongly in the commandments and was a caring lad who didn't have an angry bone in his pencil-thin body. But President Abraham Lincoln had issued a call for volunteers to save the Union and battle the rebels from the South. Weeks earlier, on April 12, 1861, the United States plunged into civil war following a Confederate attack on the federal military post Fort Sumter off the coast of Charleston, South Carolina.

"I want to fight to save our country, but I also want to honor the commandments, especially the one 'Thou shalt not kill,'" Ben told his parents.

"The commandment is better understood to mean 'you shall not murder,'" said his father. "According to the Torah, not all killing is murder. There are special circumstances when one must engage in warfare to protect the common good. Saving this country is one of them."

"Then I'm justified to fight — and kill — the rebels, right?"

"Son, there are other ways you can help the cause without killing. You could be a drummer, a medical aide, an officer's orderly, a courier. You don't necessarily have to carry a gun or shoot a cannon to serve your country."

Robert started squirming in his chair. "I, uh, have something to tell everyone." When all eyes turned to him, he cleared his throat and said, "I've joined the Seventh New York Infantry Regiment. I, uh, lied about my age."

"What?" thundered his father.

"Oh, no!" cried his mother.

"It's okay," assured Robert, who, although two years younger than Ben, was as tall as him and huskier. "I'm going to be a drummer. Nothing will happen to me. I'll be in the rear of all the action." He explained that the drums called assembly, transmitted orders, and boosted morale. The more he talked, the more understanding his parents were of his enlistment.

"Then I'll join, too," said Ben.

"Enlist as a drummer like me," Robert suggested.

"But you know how to drum. I don't know anything about drumming."

"It doesn't matter, Ben. I'll teach you enough to get by. Half the drummers who join the army don't know a flam from a paradiddle. Whatever you do, don't be a color-bearer."

"Why not? Doesn't he just carry the flag?"

"Yes, but the job is dangerous. The color-bearer — actually, he's called a color sergeant — is out in the front lines and often the first to get shot."

During the Civil War, opposing forces faced each other on battle lines across open spaces, sometimes only a few dozen yards apart. Upon command, they fired blazing volleys. While confusion and terror filled the air, the battle lines moved forward and backward and sometimes off to the side. With each volley, the blinding gray-blue gun smoke made it harder to see, and the din of cannon and gunfire often drowned out the sounds of the drums. The soldiers had to rely on the battle flags of each regiment to identify friend from foe. During the bloody havoc of combat in dense smoke, it was easy for soldiers to become confused and head the wrong way, only to be killed by the enemy or even accidentally by their own men.

"Securing a unit's colors is important," Robert explained. "Soldiers of a unit look for their regimental colors on the battlefield to rally around in all the noise and chaos. Battles are often considered lost if the colors are captured. Ben, promise me you won't be a color sergeant. The code of conduct calls for him to sacrifice his life before giving up the colors."

"I'll stick with drumming," said Ben.

Days later, he enlisted as a drummer in Company B, First New York Infantry. Before he and 849 other recruits boarded a ship for Newport News, Virginia, an army chaplain held up the American flag and told them, "Fellow soldiers, this standard of our beloved country is confided to your care. If it leads to a bloody grave, it is sweet to die for your country. If it leads to victory, you will have preserved the Constitution. This flag is the symbol of liberty, the hope of humanity. Godspeed, men!"

After the regiment arrived at Newport News, the men drilled daily and Ben learned how to drum, but he knew he wasn't good at it. A few weeks after its arrival, the regiment marched eight miles to prepare for its first battle near Big Bethel Church.

Even though he was ordered to stay in the rear, Ben was nervous. He could tell the others were, too. Everyone was quiet, lost in his own thoughts. The vast majority of the New Yorkers among the 4,400-man force had never experienced combat before.

One young soldier eager to fight was Jacob Turnbull, Ben's 17-year-old tent mate. "My trigger finger is getting real itchy," he told Ben.

"Aren't you scared?" Ben asked.

"A little. But mostly I'm excited." Jacob's first military thrill had come the night before when he was a member of a scouting mission. Finding a bucket of black paint and a brush near Bethel Church, Jacob painted DEATH TO TRAITORS! and DOWN WITH THE REBELS! on its white walls.

"It won't bother you to kill another man, someone you don't know?" Ben asked.

Jacob shook his head. "It's 'kill or be killed,' my friend." He jabbed Ben in the ribs and said, "You do the drumming, and I'll do the shooting."

At 8 A.M., Ben and his fellow drummers began a rhythmic drumbeat as the Union troops formed their battle line. When they were within a few hundred yards of the enemy's position, the Confederates opened fire. Hour after hour, the Union soldiers attempted assaults on the rebels' earthworks, but they were repelled each time.

As soldiers fell all around him, Ben dropped his drum and raced over to a farmhouse where he hitched a pony to a wagon. Silently asking God for forgiveness for violating the eighth commandment ("Thou shalt not steal"), he rode to the front lines and loaded the most seriously wounded and brought them to a field hospital in the rear. The Confederates won the five-hour battle, and the whipped Union soldiers trudged back to Newport News.

Because of his lifesaving actions in combat, Ben was made an orderly for Union general Joseph K. Mansfield, whose full white beard and wiry white hair made his head seem twice its actual size. "You're kind of scrawny," the general told him. "But what you lack in size, you make up with a good head on your shoulders."

One of Ben's major tasks was carrying dispatches between General Mansfield in Newport News and General John Wool at Fortress Monroe, a military installation in Hampton, Virginia.

The fort, built on the Chesapeake Bay, guarded the entrance to the James River.

Most every day, Ben hopped on board a steam-powered boat called the USS *Express* for the eight-mile trip to the fort. The vessel carried supplies, mail, soldiers, and ammunition. Lurking nearby, he knew, were Confederate gunboats based in nearby Portsmouth. But he felt safe, believing the rebels wouldn't dare attack the unarmed *Express* because Yankee ships and the fort were so close.

At dawn on December 29, 1861, Ben was aboard the *Express* as it towed the schooner *Sherwood*, which was full of barrels of fresh water bound for Union ships that were patrolling offshore.

"Captain!" shouted a sailor. "I see an unidentified boat off the starboard [right] side!"

Ben stepped out onto the bow (front) of the *Express* and peered into the chilly fog. Suddenly, he saw a flash of light followed by a muffled boom. Seconds later, a shell screamed overhead and slammed into the water on the port (left) side.

"It's a Rebel steamer!" another sailor yelled. "It's coming after us!"

Ben gulped. *Stay calm*, he told himself. *Don't panic.* Another shell struck the water, this time much closer. *We're defenseless*, he thought. *Our boat has no guns. All we can do is try to outrun them.*

The *Express* steamed at full power toward Fortress Monroe, but the Confederate gunship the *Sea Bird* was gaining on them.

He's closing in on us because we're too slow from towing that schooner, Ben thought. *They'll catch up to us and take us precious prisoner. I don't want to be captured.* He could feel the panic trying to seize his body. Despite the brisk morning, he was sweating and his stomach was churning. *If only we didn't have to tow that schooner.* Then it dawned on him what needed to be done. *I can't waste time seeking permission. I've got to act now!*

The *Sea Bird* was so close that the Confederates were firing their rifles at the Union sailors, forcing them to seek cover. Ben crouched low and worked his way to the stern (rear) of the *Express.* He grabbed an ax, stood up, and began chopping at the thick, heavy rope that was attached to the *Sherwood.* A bullet whizzed by his head, but the slender teen kept whacking away until the rope snapped in two, casting the schooner adrift.

Instantly, the *Express* lurched forward and picked up speed. Peeking above the gunwale (the edge of the upper side of the boat), Ben smiled. *It worked! It worked!* The distance between the *Express* and the *Sea Bird* grew wider. *We won't be prisoners after all.* But then he wondered, *Am I in trouble for causing the schooner to end up in enemy hands?*

Meanwhile, hearing the commotion, eight Union gunboats rushed to the scene to protect the *Express.* Several shots were fired at the *Sea Bird,* which was now towing the *Sherwood* to Rebel-controlled Portsmouth. The Yankee boats followed but were soon driven back by artillery from Confederate shore batteries.

When the *Express* was out of danger, the captain asked to see the person responsible for cutting loose the *Sherwood*. Ben was escorted to the bridge.

"Do you realize what you have done?" the captain asked Ben.

"Yes, sir, and I'm sorry, sir, that the enemy has captured our water boat, but I felt I had to set it free or we would have all been captured," he blurted. "Am I going to be punished?"

"Punished? Why, lad, I want to commend you. If you hadn't taken such quick action, we indeed would have been prisoners. You saved our ship and our lives."

As they reached the dock at Fortress Monroe, the men aboard the *Express* gave Ben three cheers.

"I hear that you are a hero," General Mansfield told Ben later that day. "I knew you had the heart of a smart military man inside that skinny frame of yours."

For the next six months, the private carried out his duties as a courier and orderly for the general. He returned to his role as a drummer whenever his regiment engaged in combat, which involved only a few skirmishes. However, the regiment, as part of the Union's Army of the Potomac, saw heavy fighting later that summer in what was called the 1862 Peninsula Campaign, an attempt by the Yankees to capture Richmond, the capital of the Confederacy.

On the night of June 29, members of the First New York Regiment were on picket duty, which meant they had to protect the rear as Union forces marched toward their next position.

Guarding the backside of the march while walking meant that the New Yorkers were targets for rebel sharpshooters and also for Confederate guerillas looking to capture Yankees who fell behind.

Suffering from malaria, Ben's tent mate Jacob couldn't keep up with the others. "I've got to rest," he moaned. "I can't go on anymore without taking a break. Just a few minutes."

"You can't stop, Jacob," said Ben. "We must keep marching or we'll be picked off or captured by the Rebs."

Jacob waved him off, staggered over to a tree, and slumped to the ground. "Go ahead, Ben. Just leave me here. I'll take my chances."

"I can't leave you alone." With his heavy backpack and cumbersome drum, it was impossible for Ben to carry Jacob and his equipment. "Jacob, please! You've got to keep moving!"

"I can't. I'm too weak."

In desperation, Ben unhooked his drum and then smashed it so the enemy couldn't use it. Then he picked up Jacob's musket and haversack. "Get up and lean on me, Jacob. We must get out of here right now!"

Jacob slowly stood up. He put his arm around Ben's shoulder and managed to reach the rest of the troops without becoming prey for the rebels.

At a farm near Glendale, Virginia, Confederate forces attacked the Yankees with artillery, followed by a ferocious charge. While tending to Jacob, Ben saw Lieutenant George Foster on his horse galloping straight toward him. Foster was pale, his eyes vacant. His hand was clutching his neck where blood was spurting from a large wound. As the horse ran by, the officer tumbled off his saddle and crashed to the ground.

"Lieutenant!" cried Ben, racing over to him. There was nothing the drummer could do. Foster was dead.

"Those damn Rebs!" he wailed, tears streaming down his face. *I can't stand by here in the rear any longer while everyone else is getting shot.*

He rushed to a captain near the front lines and said, "Sir, my drum has been destroyed, so I'm useless as a drummer. Let me fight with the rest of my regiment."

"Okay, boy. Go shoulder a rifle."

"Thank you, sir." Ben grabbed Jacob's weapon and joined his fellow New Yorkers on the front lines. As flying bullets zinged overhead, Ben never felt so scared — or so troubled. He tried to shoot, but his hands were trembling too much for a steady aim. He wasn't sure if it was the fear of being shot or the thought of killing someone that made him feel this frightened and anxious.

He knew the moment he pulled the trigger, he would be going against everything he felt about his own humanity, everything he had learned about the sanctity of life, everything he believed about the sixth commandment.

Just then came the order to charge. No matter how scared or troubled he was, he didn't want to show these emotions to his fellow soldiers. He rose with the others and began running forward through the smoke, haze, and bullets.

About 20 yards to his left, Charley Mahorn, one of the color bearers, was struck by a bullet in the chest. Mahorn let out an anguished cry, dropped the flag, and fell in a heap. Ben hurried over and saw him take one final breath. *Someone has to carry the colors,* Ben thought.

He grasped the flag, held it up, and joined the charge. But when the Confederates concentrated their fire on the advancing Yankees, the order was given to fall back. He spun around and spotted another dead color-bearer, the regiment's flag by his side.

Ben threw away his gun and picked up the other banner. He flung a flag over each shoulder and beat a hasty retreat for the safety of the Union line. The rebels were close behind, firing a deadly volley at the Yankees. One of the bullets struck the fleshy part of Ben's arm, but he was too scared to let the wound slow him down. Still clutching the flags, he made a mad dash for a tree line where Union soldiers were taking a stand, shooting back at the advancing enemy.

He raced into the woods and then came to a clearing where other Yankees had gathered. But he was in the wrong regiment. While searching for his unit, he came face to face with General Philip Kearny, division commander, and said, "I'm sorry, sir, but I've lost my regiment."

"I saw what you did, Private. That was quite brave, risking your life to rescue the colors. You're a born color-bearer. As general, I can make battlefield promotions, so I promote you to color sergeant. What do you have to say about that?"

"Thank you, sir. But, uh, can you tell me where the First New York Regiment is?"

"On the right flank, about a quarter mile away at Malvern Hill."

Ben hurried off, found his regiment, and turned over the flags to Colonel Garrett Dyckman. That evening when the colonel received word of Ben's promotion, he called the teen over and said, "Color Sergeant Levy, you will have the honor of carrying the regiment's colors tomorrow in battle."

"Yes, sir. Thank you, sir."

Ben didn't sleep much that night. He thought about what his brother Robert had said about color-bearers being "often the first to get shot." And Ben mulled over the color sergeant's code of conduct, which called for him to part with his life before parting with the colors.

The next morning, the New Yorkers marched along a dusty road to get in position on Malvern Hill as tens of thousands of troops on both sides readied for battle. When they neared the hill, the men in Ben's regiment were covered in so much grime that their uniforms looked more gray than blue. The regiment was crossing an open field when they unexpectedly found themselves under attack.

"Lie down, men!" ordered Colonel Dyckman. Like his fellow soldiers, Ben sprawled to the ground in the tall grass, praying the artillery that was raining down on them wouldn't land on him.

"My God!" shouted Colonel Dyckman. "We're getting shelled by our own men! They're mistaking us for Confederates!"

Turning to Ben, he yelled, "Levy! I need you to unfurl the colors, advance down the center of the field, and wave the flag until the firing ceases. It's up to you to make those Union batteries see that they're firing on their own men."

"Yes, sir!" *One, two, three,* Ben counted to himself, working up the nerve. Then he leaped to his feet and dashed toward the center of the field, wildly waving the flag. His actions worked. The shelling stopped, triggering a cheer from the New Yorkers.

Unfortunately, Ben had caught the attention not only of the Union artillerymen, but also Confederate sharpshooters, who opened fire on Ben, forcing him to dive to the ground. He held on to the flag and pulled it close to his chest. *Oh, no, what do I do now?* he wondered, curling up to make himself a smaller target. He closed his eyes. *Please stop shooting. Please.* While the rebels kept him pinned down, one of the musketballs struck the flagstaff.

Then a hard thud slammed into his hip, hurting his thigh. "Ouch!" he yelped. He felt a warm liquid trickle down both sides of his leg. *I've been shot. It must be bad because of all the blood. Do I dare look?* He opened his eyes and stared at his hip, expecting the worse. But there was no blood. Then he understood what happened and chuckled. His canteen had been shot clean through, causing the water to dribble down his leg. Although his thigh was sore, the musketball hadn't penetrated the skin.

I can't stay out here, or they'll shoot me dead, he thought. *But if I try to make a run for it, they're sure to hit me. I have one choice.*

While still curled up on the ground, he disconnected the flag from the staff. Then he tore his handkerchief into strips and used them to tie the colors into a bundle. Clutching the bundle to his chest, he twisted his body until he was parallel to his regiment and then rolled over and over until he reached his fellow soldiers. When he arrived safely, his comrades burst into cheers and laughter over his bold escape.

Accepting congratulations, the relieved teen took off his hat and wiped the sweat off his dirt-caked face. That's when he noticed two bullet holes in his hat.

Ben proudly carried the First New York's colors in battle for the remainder of his two-year enlistment and served his country bravely — and he did it without firing a shot.

After a seven-month stay at home, Ben joined the Fortieth New York Regiment and returned to combat. He was severely wounded in his left leg in 1864 and barely recovered.

In 1865, Ben became one of the first — if not the first — Jewish soldier to receive the nation's highest military award, the Medal of Honor, for his gallantry as a color-bearer during battle.

THE HERO OF LEE'S MILL

JULIAN SCOTT

"**I** was left for dead on the battlefield after a cannon recoiled violently and knocked me out. When I woke up, it was night and I was alone. My fellow soldiers had retreated to the other side of the Potomac. I discovered that a Reb had rifled through my pocket, stole my money, and took my gun.

"The Confederates were everywhere, and I was sure I would be made a prisoner if they knew I was alive. I crawled past the pickets and slid into the river, and the current carried me to a small island. I hid in a cornfield until morning. Just my luck, I had landed on an island teeming with Rebs. My luck turned good, however, later that day when a Union patrol arrived and drove the Confederates off the island."

Fifteen-year-old Julian Scott put down the letter from his older brother, Lucien, who had enlisted in the Union army days after the start of the Civil War. Every time Lucien, 18, wrote a letter home about his thrilling combat experiences, Julian became more inspired. *I have to join the army,* Julian thought. *I don't care if I am too young.* He had always been fascinated by the military. It was in his blood. His great-grandfather Jonathan Scott was a lieutenant in the Revolutionary War. His grandfather Jonathan Jr. fought against the British in the 1814 Battle of Plattsburgh. And now his big brother was a soldier in the Civil War.

On June 1, 1861, when Julian learned that a recruiting officer had arrived in Johnson, Vermont, he hurried into town and stood in line to enlist in the Third Vermont Regiment. Most of the recruits — toughened farmers and sturdy millworkers — dwarfed the slightly built five-foot four-inch teenager.

After sizing up Julian, the recruiter told him, "Sorry, boy, but you're too small to be a soldier. You aren't big enough to carry out the physically demanding duties of an infantryman."

"But I want to serve my country. I want to join the army."

"We can use eager, healthy lads like you, but not to fight. The army needs boys to signal commands as drummers, buglers, and fifers."

"If that's the only way I can get in the army," Julian said with disappointment. The recruiter handed him enlistment papers. Julian knew that because he was underage, he would need his parents' consent. *Pa is in poor health and with Lucien in the army, I'm the oldest boy at home*, Julian thought. *Pa won't give me permission.*

"Get your parents to sign, boy," said the recruiter.

"That won't be necessary, sir, because I'm sixteen," Julian lied.

Back home, he quietly packed his belongings and penned a lengthy letter to his parents, explaining that he had an obligation to serve his country just like his older brother, and that he would be careful and return home once the war was over. Then he sneaked out of the house and joined the other recruits.

As a member of Company E, Third Vermont Regiment, he was officially a fifer but also a drummer. When the regiment marched to its first major assignment — helping guard Washington, D.C. — the soldiers wore sprigs of pine affixed to their caps. Julian's oversize uniform half covered his hands, smothering the airholes of his fife whenever he played.

During his free time at the regiment's post at Fort Smith, Julian, who had an extraordinary talent for drawing, spent hours with his pencil and sketch pad capturing all facets of military life. He was especially fond of drawing portraits of his fellow Yankees who sent his pictures of them back home.

One of those soldiers was William Scott, a young private of Company K. He and Julian shared the same last name but were not related. William, always eager to please, was well liked by everyone and nice to a fault. As he sat for his portrait on the afternoon of August 30, 1861, he was munching on cherries. "I love cherries. I can eat an orchard full of 'em," he said between constant yawns.

"Why are you so tired?" Julian asked.

"A good buddy was sick last night, so I took his place for guard duty. I've been up since two this morning and I'm a little tired. And I have to pull my regular turn as a picket again tonight. But I can handle it."

An hour later, Julian finished the drawing and handed it to William. "Hoo-hee, this is a darn-near perfect likeness of my mug!" William crowed, not taking his eyes off the sketch. "Thank you. You're blessed with a great gift, Julian. You're gonna be a famous artist some day. I just know it. I'm sendin' this picture home, and when my family sees it, they'll be thrilled. They're awful proud of me."

Julian, who refused to take any money for the drawing, smiled. "I'm glad you like it, William." Praise from his fellow soldiers was enough payment for the budding artist.

Days later, drummer Bart Collins rushed over to Julian and said breathlessly, "Did you hear the news about William Scott? He was caught sleeping on picket duty a few nights ago. They court-martialed him yesterday, and he was found guilty. They're going to execute him by firing squad in four days!"

Julian was stunned. "But it's not his fault. He was up for two straight nights. Even if he is guilty, why in heaven's name would they execute him?"

"According to the Articles of War, general orders require that a sentry found asleep on duty must be shot. The army is on edge after the Confederates whipped us at Manassas [two months earlier]. The Rebs are about ten miles away, so we can't have a guard asleep at his post or else Washington could fall."

Julian felt sick to his stomach. "We've got to do something. The army can't shoot one of its own soldiers."

Bart nodded and said, "Petitions are going around asking for mercy."

Julian turned his scratch pad into a petition and hustled around the fort collecting signatures from privates, sergeants, and officers. After he handed in his petition — the soldiers had gathered 200 names — Julian prayed William's life would be spared.

On the morning of September 9, the entire brigade was called out, and several soldiers were picked for the firing squad. As one of the drummers, Julian would have to witness the execution of a good and decent comrade. William was brought out blindfolded. The condemned soldier looked deadly pale, and an occasional shudder shook his body, but he asked for no mercy. A general read the following order:

"Private William Scott, of Company K of the Third Regiment of Vermont, having been found guilty by court-martial of sleeping on his post while a sentinel on picket guard, has been sentenced to be executed by firing squad."

Julian's heart sank. *Oh, my God, the petitions failed. They're going to execute William. How can the army be so cruel? I can't stand to see this.*

The general continued, "The commanding officers of the brigade, the regiment, and the company of the command, together with many other privates and officers of his regiment, have earnestly appealed to Lieutenant General George McClellan to spare the life of the offender. The president of the United States has expressed a wish that as this is the first condemnation to death in this army for this crime, mercy may be extended to the criminal."

Julian perked up. *What? Did I hear right? The petitions reached the president, and he agrees with us!*

"This fact, viewed in connection with the inexperience of the condemned as a soldier, his previous good conduct and general good character, and the urgent pleas made on his behalf, have determined the lieutenant general to grant the pardon so earnestly prayed for. Private William Scott will be released from confinement and returned to duty. Dismissed!"

Julian and the soldiers shouted for joy and raced over to pound William on the back and shake his hand. "Three cheers for Lincoln!" Julian shouted. "Hip, hip, hooray!" He pulled out his fife and played a happy tune.

Two days later, Julian had his first taste of combat, at Lewinsville, Virginia, where Yankee troops chased off dozens of Confederate pickets. But then hundreds of Confederates, firing muskets and cannons, counterattacked. Julian crept up close to the battle lines to get a good view. He stood near a Union colonel who was on a horse, urging his men to remain calm.

As the shells exploded over them, Julian, like many of the soldiers, involuntarily ducked his head. The colonel barked at his men, "Don't cower! Hold your heads high and act like Union soldiers! We're not afraid of a few rebel shells!" Just then an 18-inch shell exploded within a few yards of him, spreading shrapnel in all directions. The colonel leaped off his horse and took cover behind a rock. After he stood up and soothed his frightened horse, he shouted to his men, "Never mind what I said. It's fine if you want to dodge the large shells!"

Laughter rippled across the battle line. Julian didn't find anything funny and headed toward the rear. That's when he saw a dead man for the first time. The Union soldier was leaning against a big tree as if asleep, but his entire chest had been blown open by a cannonball, exposing his guts. Julian only caught a glimpse of him, but it was enough to make the teenager throw up.

By April the following year, the Vermonters massed with other units in the Peninsula Campaign. As Union forces marched from the Virginia coast toward Richmond, they encountered stiff resistance from the Confederates near Lee's Mill. The enemy had constructed earthworks and rifle pits on the north bank of the Warwick River. To further block the advance, they had also built several dams so the river would be harder for the Yankees to cross.

Four companies of the Third Vermont were given the mission to capture the rifle pits, so 192 men moved into position under wooded cover for several hours, waiting to attack. The damp ground swarmed with mosquitoes, and the men swatted and scratched while exchanging sporadic fire with the enemy.

As with all military musicians, one of Julian's duties would come after the battle. He would help bring the wounded back to the field hospital. *I hope there won't be many*, he told himself.

Julian spotted William Scott and whispered, "Good luck, William."

"I've been waiting a long while to prove myself," William said. "My time has come."

Minutes later, Union batteries opened up on the Confederate rifle pits across the river. Under cover of the artillery, the Vermonters waded in the 100-yard-wide shallow river. Roots, small trees, floating debris, and underbrush made it difficult to walk in the foamy, chilly two- to four-foot-deep water.

From a safe position on the south side, Julian watched as his fellow soldiers held their leather cartridge boxes over their heads to keep the paper-wrapped ammunition dry.

When the Yankees reached halfway across the river, the rebels opened fire. Wounded men passed dry cartridges to those who had tripped and ruined their own ammo. Julian was proud to see that most of the first wave of Vermonters had made it to the opposite bank. With fixed bayonets, they charged the Confederate rifle pits, yelling wildly and shooting steadily as they ran. He couldn't help but notice that William Scott was right at the front of the assault with the leader, Captain Samuel Pingree.

Unable to halt the onrushing men in blue, the Confederates bailed out from their earthworks and took cover in the nearby thickets behind them. The Yankees quickly took control of the rifle pits, and a flag was raised, signaling for reinforcements.

"Hoo-ray!" shouted Julian. "We did it!"

But his joy turned to shock when two rebel infantry regiments rose up from behind another set of earthworks and pounced on the Vermonters with a deadly volley. Captain Pingree ordered his men to remain in the rifle pits, convinced that reinforcements would arrive any moment. But none did. Still, the Vermonters held their ground as best they could. Unfortunately, many of their cartridges and percussion caps were duds from getting wet during the river crossing.

When the orders came to withdraw, the Yankees gathered their wounded and fled to the river. But now the Warwick was much higher and swifter because the Rebels had opened the floodgates of the dam. Battling the high water and strong current, the retreating troops became easy targets for the enemy, and some were shot in the back. Others threw down their weapons, ammo, and gear and frantically swam toward the opposite bank only to get shot in their arms and legs. The Warwick began turning red with blood.

From his vantage point behind a pine tree, Julian teared up at the carnage unfolding in front of him. Boyhood friends and comrades were cut down in midstream. Wounded men screamed for help as they slipped beneath the water's surface. *I can't stand to watch this any longer,* he thought. *I've got to help them.*

Ignoring the intense fire from the opposite shore, he plunged into the swollen river and reached an unconscious, bleeding soldier. It was his father's friend John Backum, a large man who had been shot in the chest. Backum was too heavy for Julian to carry so the teen summoned 17-year-old Private Ephraim Brown. "Help me get him back to shore," Julian pleaded.

Ephraim took hold of Backum's right side while Julian held his left and pulled his father's friend closer to the bank. But then Ephraim screamed in pain and went under the water. He surfaced and bawled, "I've been shot in the back!"

As bullets struck the water like hailstones in a pond, Julian yanked and dragged Backum to shore where other soldiers pulled him to safety. Then Julian charged back into the water and retrieved Ephraim.

Without catching his breath, Julian splashed into the river again and spotted William Scott, who was pulling two unconscious Yankees across, barely able to keep their heads above water. "Let me help you!" shouted Julian.

Together, they brought the men to the bank. Seeing that William was bleeding from wounds in the arm and torso, Julian said, "You've been shot!"

"I'll be all right," said William. "Just flesh wounds." He spun around and ran into the Warwick to assist a wounded officer.

Feeling a surge of courage and strength that he never knew he had, Julian repeatedly jumped into the water, grabbing and dragging to safety more wounded comrades, most weighing 50 to 75 pounds more than him. Ignoring the flying bullets, he twice managed to reach the Confederate side to rescue fallen men.

He found Captain Pingree, one of the last Yankees left in the rifle pit, still firing his gun defiantly at the enemy. The captain's right thumb had been blown off, and his left shoulder was bleeding badly.

"Get out of here, Captain!" Julian shouted. He took off his neckerchief and wrapped it around the bloody stump on the officer's injured hand. Then he and another soldier hustled Pingree away and ferried him across the river.

Julian was at midstream when Sergeant Adam Nichols waved to him for help. Nichols was holding up an unconscious comrade who had been shot several times. Julian sloshed over to them and brought the injured soldier to shore. Others then carried him out of the line of fire and laid him in the grass.

Totally exhausted, Julian fell to his knees and took a couple of deep breaths. Incredibly, despite the intense gunfire, he hadn't been shot, although his face, hands, and legs were deeply scratched from submerged tree branches and floating logs. He looked at the enemy's side of the river. The only Yankees left were sprawled on the bank, motionless.

Turning around, he stared at the last man he helped bring out. Several soldiers had crowded around their prone comrade. "He was nearly across the stream when the Rebs concentrated their fire on him," said Nichols. "He's been shot all to pieces."

Julian glanced at the wounded soldier. His bloody, swollen face looked familiar. "Who is he?"

"William Scott."

Julian winced. "Oh, no. That's so unfair. After all he's been through."

They put William on a stretcher and brought him to a field hospital where a doctor examined him and said, "He's a strong young man, but his chances don't look good."

The next morning Julian and several others went into William's tent and stood around his cot. "Boys," William rasped,

"I shall never see another battle. Tell the folks at home that I tried to do the right thing." His voice grew weaker with each sentence. "If you get the chance, tell President Lincoln that I tried to be a good soldier and true to the flag. I'm grateful he gave me the chance to fall like a soldier in battle and not as a coward in front of a firing squad. Good-bye, boys."

William closed his eyes, crossed his hands across his bullet-riddled chest, and took his final breath. Men who had seen friends die beside them or skirted death themselves, wept like children. *Now I know how a brave man dies*, thought Julian.

Julian knew that William would have been content to be buried in the same grave as the other fallen comrades. But Julian thought of a better place. William's body was carried to a small grove of cherry trees in the rear of the camp. At the foot of a noble oak, they dug his grave and laid him with his gear and rifle. Deep into the oak tree, they carved the initials W.S. and underneath wrote A BRAVE SOLDIER.

In a haze from exhaustion, Julian ambled around the camp, his mind a blur as he tried to relive the events of the last 24 hours. Nearly half of the Vermonters in the battle were either dead or seriously wounded.

A gravelly voice broke his concentration. "Hey, you're the boy who ran into the river and saved our men."

Julian turned around and faced Lieutenant Colonel Wheelock Veazey. "Yes, sir," said Julian. "I couldn't sit still and watch them die out there without trying."

"My aide counted the number of soldiers you helped rescue. It was at least nine. For a boy, you showed some man-size courage. You ran yourself into unnecessary danger time and again to assist your fellow man in the thick of enemy fire. Many owe their lives to you. I won't forget your bravery."

"Thank you, sir."

Two months later, the Vermonters fought the rebels nonstop in what was known as the Seven Days' Battle. They clashed in towns, forests, and fields; across rivers, hills, and swampland. They engaged in combat during the day and marched during the night. They fought not only the Confederates, but also fatigue, disease, and lice.

Paying little heed to bullets and artillery shells, Julian repeatedly carried and dragged wounded men from the battle lines to field hospitals. Often he was pressed into service as a surgeon's assistant, helping lift severely wounded soldiers onto the amputating bench. He tried to calm each patient as the surgeon hastily placed a cattle horn over the soldier's mouth to administer chloroform to anesthetize him. But sometimes the patient didn't receive enough of the anesthetic and threw himself wildly about while the doctor amputated. Julian helped dig holes to bury the pile of amputated legs — many with shoes and socks still on them — and arms.

During the Battle of White Oak Swamp on June 30, shrapnel whistled overhead, panicked army horses bolted for the rear, and splinters of pine trees flew through the air from artillery explosions. During the melee, Sergeant Nichols's leg was nearly blown off. Julian helped Nichols, who used his gun as a crutch, toward the rear.

"Look out for that sniper over there," the sergeant rasped. About 50 yards away from behind a tree crouched a rebel. Julian laid Nichols down and took the sergeant's gun. Suddenly, Julian felt a stinging impact in his right hip, causing his leg to buckle. He tumbled to the ground and screamed in pain. The teenager's hip felt like it was on fire. "I'm shot," he groaned. Then he passed out.

Julian had suffered a serious wound and was transported to a hospital on David's Island near New York, where most of the men required months of care.

For weeks, Julian smelled the sickening odor of disease as comrades lay on iron cots atop chamber pots. The wards were punctuated by screams of pain. Every day, the soldiers who had died were removed, and their empty beds were quickly filled with endless casualties.

When he was able to limp and move about, Julian toted slop buckets, changed bandages, and comforted the dying. To raise the spirits of his comrades, he sketched their likenesses with charcoal or chalk on the whitewashed walls over their beds. Sometimes, he created lively battlefield scenes.

One day, Julian was sketching a portrait of a middle-age soldier who had lost both legs. "Say, I know you," said the soldier. "You were that boy hero at Lee's Mills. I was there. I was shot in the shoulder, and you helped me get across the river. How about drawing a scene on the wall of that day?"

Julian shook his head. "I can't," he replied in a somber voice. "Some scenes I witnessed are just too painful to draw — and that's one of them. Too many of my friends died that day."

"Maybe so," said the soldier. "But even more would have died if it hadn't been for you."

Julian's drawings at the hospital caught the eye of Vermont businessman Henry Clark who often visited patients to cheer them up. Clark was so impressed with Julian's artistic talents that, after Julian's discharge from the army, the businessman helped the teenager gain admission to a prestigious art school, the National Academy of Design.

Julian soon returned to the front lines, but this time as an artist, and created realistic paintings fully documenting battle scenes and the everyday life of soldiers in combat. After the war, he painted scenes of Native Americans. By the time Julian died at the age of 55 on July 4, 1901, in Plainfield, New Jersey, he was one of the leading American artists of his time. He was survived by a wife and daughter.

Although hailed for his artistic skills, Julian achieved the respect of the military for his bravery during combat. In 1865, he was awarded the Army's highest award — the Medal of Honor — for "the gallant conduct" he displayed at Lee's Mill when he crossed the river "under a terrific fire of musketry several times to assist in bringing off the wounded."

THE SOUTH'S BRAVEST LADS

⭐

VIRGINIA MILITARY INSTITUTE
CORPS OF CADETS

On the night of May 10, 1864, the young cadets of Virginia Military Institute were awakened from their sleep by drums playing the long roll — the traditional signal of an enemy attack and for troops to line up.

When they assembled on the parade grounds, Major Tom Williamson announced in a booming voice, "Cadets, you are ordered to appear here at four o'clock in the morning with canteens, haversacks, and blankets for a two-day march to Staunton." The town was 36 miles north of the VMI campus, which was in Lexington.

"General [John C.] Breckinridge needs your help in repelling more than six thousand Yankees who are advancing down the Shenandoah Valley. This is your opportunity to aid the

Confederate cause and make this a shining moment in VMI history."

At first, his words were met with stunned silence. Then when the cadets were dismissed, the air exploded with wild cheering. "Our time has come at last!" shouted Cadet William Cabell.

The famed military school had nearly 300 cadets, most of them teenagers, some as young as 14. Half were first-year students, or "rats" as the upperclassmen called them. The corps of cadets included the sons of Virginia professionals, the wealthy, and the powerful as well as those on scholarships from poor families. The school offered a full range of academic courses as well as military studies.

During the first few years of what it called the War Between the States, the Confederacy chose to keep the cadets in class rather than on the battlefield, even though they were eager to fight. In fact, in March 1864, at a mass meeting, the cadets passed a resolution offering their services to General Robert E. Lee. Although he was moved by their gesture, he declined. The cadets continued their studies while drilling and participating in war games in preparation for a life in the military after graduation. They had always hoped to experience combat . . . and now, two months after their offer to fight, it looked like they finally might get their chance.

General Franz Sigel of the Union Army and his 6,300 men planned to cut a major supply line to General Lee's troops and to Richmond. It was up to General Breckinridge's undermanned southwestern Virginia force of 4,000 to stop him. The Confederate troops needed all the help they could get, including the assistance of the young men of VMI.

At 7 A.M. on May 11, more than 250 cadets in four companies shouldered their Austrian-made muzzle loaders, checked their 40 rounds of ammunition, and paraded on the avenue. Joining them were artillery crews with two cannons, a fifer, two drummers, and seven field and staff officers led by Colonel Scott Shipp, who was only 24 years old. They marched out of Lexington, leaving behind 27 disappointed cadets who were ordered to guard the institute.

With full packs, the teenage student soldiers slogged north in the muddy road to face their destiny. Each was lost in his own thoughts.

Moses Ezekiel felt excited and scared. His mother had sent him to VMI to learn the arts of war, because she wanted a son who would fight for his home and country. Although he was tough, Moses had trouble adapting to the military academy and was ranked at the bottom of his class.

With every step he took, Jenner Jones, 17, grew bolder. He couldn't wait to experience combat so he could avenge the death of his eldest brother who died in the Battle of Seven Pines in 1862. John Wise, the 15-year-old son of the former governor of Virginia, also sought revenge against the Union because his big brother, Jennings, died in a battle on Roanoke Island.

Willie McDowell, 17, was thinking about Major Williamson's two cute teenage daughters. Several weeks earlier, Willie had fainted during a dress parade and was carried to the major's house nearby. There, the major's daughters revived Willie by putting water on his face and rubbing his temples. The next day, they sent a note to him asking about his health. "When we return from battle, I'm going to visit with those pretty girls," he told fellow cadet Samuel "Frank" Atwill during the march.

"If this is the way one gets rewarded for fainting at dress parade, I'll pretend to faint, too," Frank whispered to Willie. "But when I do, I'll have someone next to me rub chalk on my face and hands so I look sick, and then take me to Major Williamson's."

Willie laughed. "Frank, those sweet lassies don't want to see a donkey like you." Puffing out his chest, he added, "They want to see a stallion like me."

After walking for two days in thick mud and a drenching rain, they arrived at Staunton, where other Confederate forces were gathering. As the cadets passed by the battle-scarred Sixth Virginia Regiment, the veterans taunted the teenagers. They jeered and whistled at the cadets, calling them wagon dogs — an insulting term meaning soldiers who pretend to be sick to avoid combat — and parlor soldiers — men who dress for show rather than war. "Hey, goobers. When you grow up, then you can wear uniforms!" shouted one veteran. "Watch 'em run to Mama when the hornets [slang for bullets] come flyin' at 'em!" yelled another soldier.

Not accustomed to being teased, the cadets became indignant and were ready to fight the veterans when Colonel Shipp moved them on and set up camp a quarter mile away.

Over the next two days, the cadets and Breckinridge's men hiked another 35 miles before camping south of New Market, a sleepy town of 700 persons. The Union forces were only a few miles away, arriving from the north.

That night, the cadets couldn't get to sleep. Their minds were whirring with thoughts of battle and blood, and feelings of fear and fervor. Even if they could sleep, they didn't get much. About 1 A.M. on Sunday, May 15, in the rainy darkness, they were quietly awakened. After a prayer by Captain Frank Preston, the cadets trekked silently until they reached a rambling farm outside of New Market at dawn.

The thunder rumbled and the lightning crackled during heavy showers that pelted the soldiers as they took their positions. Days of rain had turned much of the farmland where the battle would be fought into deep, gushy mud. Breckinridge ordered the cadets and the Twenty-sixth Virginia Battalion, made up of much older men, held in reserve. "What? We have to stay behind with the schoolboys?" protested one member of the battalion. His other comrades complained, too — and loud enough for the cadets to hear.

"I've had enough!" growled Oliver Evans to his fellow students. "How many want to go into battle?" Everyone cheered. The hulking six-foot two-inch cadet said, "Then I'll ask Colonel Shipp to plead our case to the general."

Shipp went to Breckinridge, but the general was firm in wanting to hold out the cadets and the Twenty-sixth Virginia and use them as a rear guard.

By midmorning, as rain continued to fall, the artillery began drowning out the thunder, signaling the start of a brutal battle that would be waged over rolling hills, a field of mud, and a dense orchard. The rebels advanced on the Yankees who were dug in on the slopes of a hill, but heavy musketry and artillery sent many Confederates to a quick death and pushed their comrades back. Shouting out orders from his horse, Breckinridge quickly called in the Twenty-sixth Virginia to fill in for the casualties. But their presence on the battlefield fell short of what was needed.

"General, there aren't enough veterans to hold off the Yankee line!" reported Major Charles Semple. "There's a gap in our line that has to be filled."

The general closed his eyes and took two deep breaths. "Then put in the boys, and may God forgive me." The general bowed in anguish until his forehead touched his horse's neck.

When word reached the cadets to prepare for battle, John Wise and three of his comrades were ordered to guard the wagons in the rear. But there was no way he was staying behind. "If I should return home and tell my father that I was on the baggage guard when the cadets were in battle, I know what my fate would be," John told his fellow cadets. "He would kill me with ridicule, which is worse than bullets. I intend to join the fight. Come on, you want to join me?" He picked up his musket and raced to catch up with the rest of the corps. The other three baggage guards joined him, leaving the task of protecting the supply wagons to an elderly African-American man who had traveled with the troops.

Learning he was going into battle, Cadet Porter Johnson quickly stuffed his left-front shirt pocket with several letters from home because he wanted to keep them close to his heart in case he should die. He also shoved into the same breast pocket two squares of hardtack — a tough-to-bite cracker made of flour and water — to stave off hunger.

After the fifer and drummers struck up a tune, the VMI Corps of Cadets lined up shoulder to shoulder at the center of the Confederate line and then marched over the crest of Shirley's Hill. Across the way on Manor's Hill, the Yankees blasted their artillery while their infantry fired away. Three Union batteries — each with six cannons — were trained on the attackers.

In the first wave, the seasoned Confederates hustled down Shirley's Hill, and the boys from VMI followed. Unfortunately, the cadets failed to receive the order to run to the bottom to minimize exposure to the Union's cannons. Instead, the cadets marched down the slope in dress-parade fashion in perfect order even though they were within range of the enemy.

His golden hair flopping in the rain, Oliver Evans proudly carried the VMI colors in front of his fellow cadets. He would glance back and wink at his good friend Porter Johnson who was inspired by Oliver's obvious excitement. Oliver's face was wreathed in smiles. To Porter, Oliver's whole body seemed to grow as he carried that banner with such glory.

Suddenly, an artillery shell struck the ground near them and exploded. The force knocked Oliver down, but he quickly jumped to his feet. However, the same blast turned Porter Johnson 180 degrees and slammed him into the mud while his gun flew over his head. A piece of shrapnel struck just over his heart, tearing a huge hole in his jacket and shirt and ripping a gash on his chest.

Porter gasped, fearing the worst. But then he realized how incredibly lucky he was. The letters and hardtack he had stuffed in his shirt pocket had kept the shrapnel from piercing his heart, saving his life. He stuck a handkerchief over the wound and got up to look for his gun. But then, following another explosion, a second piece of shrapnel struck him on the left arm, smacking him back to the ground. He was in such shock that, at first, he thought his arm was torn off at the shoulder. Thankfully, his arm was still there although it was completely paralyzed and scorched from shoulder to elbow. He staggered to the rear where he was treated at the field hospital.

Another shell exploded in the middle of John Wise's company. Fire flashed, the earth rocked, the sky whirled around. John stumbled, and his gun pitched forward. Jolted by the pain, he fell to his knees, his head covered in blood.

William Cabell gave John a look of pity. But there was no slowing down to help a fallen comrade. William turned away and called out to the others, "Close up, men!"

Determining he wasn't seriously hurt, John wiped the blood from his forehead, found his weapon, and rejoined the fray.

The cadets took cover in a slight ravine dotted with cedar scrub and stumps. There, they shed their blankets and other gear so they would be carrying a lighter load in case of hand-to-hand combat.

As the Confederates resumed their march toward the Union guns, the cadets were shocked by what they saw in front of them. The officers of the Twenty-sixth Virginia had to force at gunpoint a few reluctant, scared soldiers — including some who earlier had insulted the cadets — to move forward.

The combatants on both sides had trouble seeing through the smoke and cascading rain, and hearing orders over the deafening noise. No one could tell the difference between the constant claps of thunder and the roar of more than 30 cannons booming at the same time.

A deadly artillery shell blew up directly in front of cadets William Cabell, Jenner Jones, and Charles Crockett, killing them instantly. Seconds later, Willie McDowell was fatally shot through the heart.

John Wise ran over to Willie and felt like crying. His good friend, a slightly built North Carolinian who had just turned 16, lay on his back as if he were asleep. Before Willie died, he had torn open his jacket and shirt, and now, even in death, he still clutched back his clothes, exposing his gaping mortal wound.

On his way to rejoining the cadets' line, John spotted the mangled body of Jenner Jones and thought, *At least he can rest in peace with his brother.*

By now, the line was moving at a determined pace even though the muck was so thick it sucked the shoes right off the feet of several cadets. (It would later become known as the "Field of Lost Shoes.") But they kept advancing.

Colonel Shipp never looked so pale. Sweat mixed with rain rolled off his face in great drops as he barked out orders. The cadets knew he was as afraid as they were. But he inspired them because he showed them that the bravest are those who hold true to duty and honor despite tremendous fear.

As the Rebel line drew closer to the Yankees, Union General Franz Sigel had his artillery double their guns with grapeshot and canister. The air was filled with murderous small iron balls, forcing the Fifty-first Virginia Regiment on the cadets' left flank and the Sixty-second Virginia Regiment on their right to fall back. The Yankees, sensing the Rebels were reeling, launched a counterattack. But the VMI Corps of Cadets quickly moved in to fill the wide gap at the most critical moment of the battle. They did not falter even though they suffered their greatest number of casualties at this point. As the cadets passed by fallen Rebels, some of the wounded cheered them on. The teenage corps continued its steady advance through the shoe-stealing mud, in the driving rain, and under deadly fire. When anyone was killed or wounded, the gaps in the ranks were filled automatically as if nothing unusual had happened. At no time did the cadets' battle line waver.

The young soldiers ran forward to the remains of a demolished rail fence on the edge of the orchard. There they lay down behind the fence, and began — for the *first* time — to fire upon the enemy.

The battle had reached a turning point. The Confederates

were hunkered down, and the Union attack had failed. The next move would likely determine the outcome of this dreadful fight. In the swirling smoke and torrential rain, Breckinridge ordered the cadets to lead a full-scale charge on the Yankee batteries.

Colonel Shipp shouted to the cadets, "Fix bayonets!" No sooner had he uttered the command than he was struck in the chest by a shell fragment. After lying breathless on the ground for several minutes, he rose to his feet. Then he called out to his young corps, "Follow my lead, boys!"

Greeted with wild, enthusiastic yelling, the teenage soldiers rallied behind Shipp and the colors that were raised high by Oliver Evans. Eager to charge the enemy, they hardly slowed down to load and shoot their old-fashioned muzzle-loading muskets. Angry storm clouds had grown so dark that the flashes from the cannons lit up the cadets' faces.

Like several of his fellow cadets, Frank Atwill was having trouble with his weapon. The rain had swollen the wooden ramrod so that he couldn't withdraw it to reload. But he charged ahead anyway, planning on using his bayonet. "I'm gonna carve up some Yankee meat!"

Just then, he was cut down by back-to-back shots to his left leg and he crumpled in a heap. Rather than cry out in pain, he shouted to his buddies, "Go get 'em! I'll catch up with you later!" He ripped his handkerchief in two and used the pieces to wrap a tourniquet around his thigh to slow the bleeding before he lost consciousness.

Lieutenant Carter Berkeley was giving orders when he heard the cries of Cadet James Merritt. "Sir, get me a doctor. My friend is badly wounded!"

James was leaning against a tree stump, cradling Cadet J. B. Stanard whose bloodied and scorched body lay across James's legs. Drawing nearer, the officer saw that James had been shot in the stomach but was so concerned about his buddy that he hadn't even mentioned being seriously wounded himself.

The lieutenant checked J. B.'s pulse and said to James, "My poor boy, your friend is dead. You're the one who needs help. I'll get a doctor for you."

The Confederate regiments that earlier were forced to fall back had regrouped behind the cadets, who were now running toward a Union battery while the Yankees were trying to move their cannons to the rear. Rebel fire killed many of the Union horses and disabled one cannon. Unable to stop the swarming cadets, the Yankees fled in confusion, leaving behind their cannons, wounded, and dead. Soon the entire Union force was retreating with the Confederates in hot pursuit.

Cadet Hugh Fry chased down a heavyset Union officer, who had been shot in the leg. "Give up and turn over your sword," Hugh commanded.

"I refuse to surrender my sword to a child," sneered the officer.

"I'm man enough to shoot you with my gun and then run you through with my bayonet," Hugh retorted. "How do you want to die?"

The officer reluctantly handed over his sword and joined other Yankees who grumbled in shame about being captured by "a bunch of schoolboys."

Two miles away, the whipped Union forces scrambled across the north fork of the Shenandoah River and then burned the bridge behind them to prevent the pursuing rebels from capturing them.

Meanwhile, Oliver Evans hopped on the captured cannon and triumphantly waved VMI's flag, triggering ecstatic cheers from his fellow cadets, who were sopping wet, exhausted, and hungry. The joy on their faces — filthy from gunpowder and mud — knew no bounds. They whooped and hollered and kicked up their heels. Recognizing the courageous effort of the cadets, the veteran rebels who had taunted them earlier were now shouting out hearty words of approval. Even the heavens seemed to reflect their mood because the terrible rainstorm ended.

After the battle, Moses Ezekiel — in bare feet because he lost his shoes and socks in the mud — helped recover the dead and wounded. One of the first cadets he found was Frank Atwill, who had just regained consciousness.

"Did . . . we . . . win?" Frank asked in a weak, halting voice.

"We whupped 'em good," Moses replied.

Looking at his bloody leg, Frank forced a smile and said, "This should win me some sympathy from the Williamson girls when I get back to VMI."

Moses then wandered the battlefield with Cadet B. A. Colonna, searching for their mutual friend, Cadet Thomas

Jefferson, a descendant of the third U.S. president of the same name. They found him slumped by a tree, gasping for breath, his hands over a deep chest wound. Moses rushed into New Market and arranged for an ambulance wagon to pick up Tom and take him to a nearby home.

While Tom squirmed in bed in agony for the next two days, Moses tended to him, believing there was a chance the severely wounded cadet would recover. At Tom's request, Moses, who was Jewish, read from the New Testament to Tom, a Christian. On Tuesday evening, Moses read by candlelight to his friend who had requested a specific passage from the Bible (John 14:2): "In my Father's house are many mansions. If it were not so, I would have told you. I go to prepare a place for you."

As Tom's fevered mind became muddled, he thought Moses was his mother, and then his sister. He soon lost his eyesight and asked for more light. Moses realized all hope was lost. He held Tom in his arms and watched him die.

Tom was one of 10 cadets — all teenagers — who gave their lives at New Market. Frank Atwill was another. He died two months later in the hospital. The other dead included Alva Hartsfield, Luther Haynes, and Joseph Wheelwright. An additional 47 cadets were wounded. Of John Wise's three fellow baggage guards, one died and two sustained serious injuries. Overall, the Union suffered 840 casualties; the Confederates 540.

The day after the battle, General Breckinridge made a point to praise the cadets. From atop his horse, he told them, "It almost broke my heart to see boys dropping and the gaps torn in your line by the terrible fire. But the way you closed up and went after the Yankee guns was the most glorious thing I have ever seen in war. Boys, the work you did yesterday will make you famous."

Cadet Dave Pierce spoke up. "Pardon me, General, for what I'm about to say. Fame is all right. But we like our fame sandwiched with bacon and hardtack. For God's sake, we're hungry. Where is your commissary wagon?"

The general made sure the cadets got their rations within the hour.

Later that day, Cadet Sandy Stuart walked over to Lieutenant Carter Berkeley and told him, "The blot on the institute was wiped out yesterday by the best blood of Virginia."

"Cadet, I never knew there was a blot on the institute."

"Yesterday morning, your men tried to put a stigma on us by calling us wagon dogs and other insulting things."

The officer laughed. "My men were only joking. They razz one another all the time because it's part of military life. On the battlefield, those men saw what you cadets are made of, and they're all proud of every one of you — as is the whole Confederacy."

In his battle report, Colonel Scott Shipp wrote of the VMI cadets, "The boys fought like tigers and earned the admiration of friends and foes."

He was right. Years after the battle, Union captain Franklin E. Town, who fought against the cadets at the Battle of New Market, wrote: "History abounds in records of attacks [that] stir the blood and command the admiration of all who can appreciate manhood and chivalry and heroism. But these tales are expected to be written of veterans, seasoned to battle in many campaigns. However, the charge [at New Market] was made by a battalion of young lads, boys who earned their spurs of knighthood before their chins sprouted beards. As a military spectacle, it was most beautiful, and as a deed of war it was most grand.

"I don't believe the history of war contains the record of a deed more chivalrous, more daring, or more honorable than the charges of these boys to victory."

The Battle of New Market has become part of the history of Virginia Military Institute. Every year on May 15, the corps of cadets performs a special ceremony on the campus. The name of each cadet who lost his life that fateful day in 1864 is called, and a representative from the same company in today's corps answers, "Died on the field of honor, sir."

THE BABY-FACED LIEUTENANT

★

REGINALD ST. JOHN BEARDSWORTH BATTERSBY

Lanky 14-year-old British schoolboy St. John Battersby
studied the ad in the *Manchester Evening News* as if it were
speaking to him: "The day has come for you, young man — the
great day of decision! Will you fight for your king and country,
or will you hide in the safety of your home? England awaits
your answer at the nearest recruiting office. GO!"

Great Britain needed all the help it could get after declaring
war in 1914 against Germany, which had invaded Belgium and
France, triggering World War I. (The United States would join
the conflict on the side of England three years later.)

St. John turned to his friend, 14-year-old Horace Isles, and
said, "I wish I could join, but I'm way too young."

"I haven't told my parents yet, but I enlisted yesterday."

"You did? How?"

"The recruiting sergeant asked me my age, and when I told him the truth he said, 'You had better go out, come in again, and tell me different.' I came back, told him I was eighteen, and I was in."

"So they don't care what your age is as long as you lie?" asked St. John.

"The army is desperate for troops," replied Horace, a stocky redheaded teenager with peach fuzz on his upper lip.

On January 30, 1915 — a month shy of his fifteenth birthday and four months after his mother had died from an illness — St. John walked into a recruiting office. "I want to enlist in the Royal Army," he declared.

The sergeant studied the tall but slender lad and asked, "How old are you?"

Looking him straight in the eye, St. John lied, "I'm eighteen, going on nineteen."

Later that day, St. John returned home, which was in the rectory of Holy Trinity Church where his dad, Walter, was the vicar. "Father, forgive me but I lied about my age so I could join the army. I'm now a private in the Manchester Regiment."

Walter leaped to his feet and shouted in alarm, "What? A private you say? No! I will not allow it!"

"But, Father, I want to fight for our king and country. Please, you must let me go. They need all the soldiers they can get."

Walter held up his hands in surrender. "I'm not happy about you joining the army because you're so young. But I understand your desire. However, you shouldn't serve as a lowly private.

You're bright, fit, and mature for your age. You should be an officer."

"But I'm only fourteen."

"Tut, tut. Leave that to me." Over the next few days, the vicar convinced several powerful friends, including the lord mayor of Manchester and the headmaster of St. John's school, to help his son. In letters they wrote to the War Office, they lied about the boy's age and recommended he be made an officer. The conspiracy worked. Just days after St. John turned 15, he was commissioned a second lieutenant — the youngest in the army, although no one knew it at the time.

With his secret intact, he trained for a year before joining one of Britain's most famous units — the East Lancashire Regiment's Eleventh Battalion. The unit was called the Accrington Pals because so many of the soldiers in the battalion came from the town of the same name. In the spring of 1916, shortly after his sixteenth birthday, St. John and more than 700 Accrington Pals were shipped to France, joining the beleaguered French in an effort to beat back the Germans.

The teenager was given command of a platoon of 60 soldiers, from boys hiding their true age, like Horace, to men older than this father. St. John had to constantly put up with jokes about his baby-face appearance and questions about his age, but he handled those uncomfortable moments by laughing them off. He took his commission seriously and eventually gained the confidence of his men.

During the Great War, as the conflict was called, many battles were fought from complex, interlocking trenches hand-dug 8 to 12 feet deep. The sides were strengthened by sandbags, wooden frames, and wire mesh while the muddy bottom was usually covered by wooden planks called duckboards. Tunnels and dugouts were burrowed deep into the sides for greater protection from bombs and artillery shells.

The area between the German and British trenches — typically between 100 and 300 yards — was called no-man's-land, which is where most soldiers were killed or wounded.

On April 28, the Accrington Pals took over a stretch of frontline trenches between the villages of Beaumont Hamel and Serre. Despite his training, St. John wasn't prepared for the shocking horrors and terrible conditions of trench warfare. When he and his unit arrived in the trenches, he gagged from the sickening stench that smothered the area. The stomach-churning smell from nearby shallow graves, overflowing latrines, and the body odor of men who hadn't bathed in weeks mixed with the stink of rotting sandbags, stagnant mud, and cigarette smoke.

Like most soldiers, St. John eventually got used to it, mostly because they all faced more serious problems such as sniper fire, artillery shelling, and disease.

The unit's first fatalities in action came the following night when the right side of the battalion line was bombarded by enemy artillery fire. An explosion rocked the trench, causing a wall to cave in and bury several men alive. St. John rushed to the rubble and, joining others, frantically scraped away at the earth with his small field shovel until he felt a cold hand in the muddy dirt.

"I found someone!" he shouted. Careful not to injure the soldier, St. John and two others used their hands to hollow out airspace so the buried victim could breathe. But they were too late. The soldier had suffocated.

St. John now understood a harsh combat lesson: No one was safe. He saw that death or injury could happen at any time and any place, whether he was writing a letter in a trench, sleeping inside a dugout, or carrying out a mission in no-man's-land.

Death didn't always ride in on a bullet or shell. Soldiers suffered from parasites and common but dangerous infections such as dysentery, typhus, and cholera that often went untreated because there were few antibiotics. Tens of thousands of soldiers became casualties from disease during the four-year war. St. John was struck with illness more than once.

He and his comrades suffered from infestations of lice, which bred in their clothes that went unwashed for weeks at a time. Even when clothes were cleaned, the eggs lay hidden in the seams only to hatch hours later when warmed by the soldiers' body heat. Lice caused trench fever, a disease that began with severe pain followed by a high fever. Recovery took up to three months.

Because the trenches were often filled with knee-high water and mud from frequent rains, the men suffered from trench foot, a fungal infection caused by cold, wet, and unsanitary conditions. The victims' feet became cramped, swollen, bloated, and painfully tender. Walking was almost impossible, and several men were sent to the hospital as stretcher cases. St. John avoided trench foot by rubbing smelly whale oil on his feet and ankles.

If battling the Germans and disease weren't bad enough, St. John and his comrades had to fend off thousands of rats, many the size of cats. He lost count of the times he was awakened by a rat scampering across his face or the number of rodents he clubbed or stabbed to death. Also giving him the willies were the millions of cockroaches and horned beetles that swarmed in the trenches.

He kept his focus as best he could on the real enemy. One time, St. John and three of his men went on a night mission to repair barbed wire that had been ripped apart by artillery. It was a moonless, still night, and the sound carried so well that he could hear German soldiers speaking softly in their trench 100 yards away. While he and his men were working on the wire, the enemy abruptly fired several star shells — flares that lit up the sky.

"Everybody, down!" St. John whispered. He and the others low-crawled to the nearest shell crater and hid. On his back, St. John gazed at the brightened sky and for a brief moment he forgot about the war. To him, the star shells looked like lanterns hanging from a black velvet ceiling. Had this been anywhere but here, he would have uttered *oohs* and *aahs*.

He and his men waited for nearly two hours before the last of the star shells burned out. Tapping the others on the leg, he signaled for them to return to their trench. Suddenly, he heard voices murmuring in German. Judging from the sounds, they were heading straight for the bomb crater. *I refuse to get captured*, he told himself. "Don't move," he whispered to his comrades. His hands wet from sweat, St. John pulled out a hand grenade and tossed it in the direction of the voices.

Seconds later, an ear-ringing explosion rocked the ground and showered him with dirt. "Run for it!" he ordered. As German machine guns opened fire, the trio bolted out of the crater and dashed in the darkness safely back to their trench.

In May, the battalion moved from the stinky, muddy trenches to a camp in the woods in the rear of the lines where the soldiers slept in dry tarpaulin huts. St. John took his first decent shower in nearly three months — never had one felt so good — and thoroughly laundered his clothes, killing lice by the hundreds. Morale was as cheery as the blooming spring flowers.

St. John stopped by to chat with Horace Isles, who was writing a letter home. "I got another letter from my sister," Horace said. He looked around to make sure no one else was in earshot and whispered, "This is the third time she's written me, begging me to admit I'm only sixteen so the army will send me home."

"Do you want to go home?" St. John asked.

"I sure don't want to be here," said Horace. Sighing, he added, "But I made a pledge to fight for my king and country, so that's what I'll do. What about you?"

"I want to win this war. We have a tough job to do, Horace. If we all fail, there won't be much of a home to return to." He gave a wink and a nod. "We'll win this thing, and then we can go back to being boys again."

"And playing football and cricket."

Throughout June, the soldiers trained and drilled in preparation for a major attack involving 120,000 British troops. The objective: Force the Germans from their trenches in the Somme Valley and out of nine French villages in the area. The Accrington Pals would be responsible for securing the enemy's trench line in front of the fortified hilltop village of Serre, which was giving the Germans a commanding view of no-man's-land.

For six days and nights, British and French artillery fired 1.6 million shells onto the German front lines in the valley. On June 30, St. John and other Accrington Pals officers were called to a meeting headed by Captain Henry Riley.

"Tomorrow morning at seven twenty, we will go over the top and lay down in position while the German lines get shelled once again," Riley explained. "Then we will stand up, march across no-man's-land, kill or capture what few survivors remain, and take control of the German trenches. The Pals will make an orderly, parade-ground march, five yards between each man, rifles held at high port [aimed upward], in four successive waves of infantry, with one hundred eighty men in each wave."

Itching for action, St. John volunteered to lead his platoon in the first wave. "We have yet to make our mark in the war," he said. "My men are ready and eager."

"I'm sure they are, Lieutenant," the captain agreed. "Then your platoon shall be the first over the top."

"Thank you, sir," said St. John. "If I might ask, Captain, why are we going to walk instead of run across no-man's-land?"

"Commander [Sir Henry] Rawlinson doesn't want to tire out the men or cause them to hurt themselves by rushing across a field pockmarked with craters and holes. This should be a fairly easy task. No one could have survived the shellacking we gave them the past week — which was the heaviest bombardment in history."

Returning to his platoon, St. John could hardly contain his excitement when he broke the news to his men. "We're going over the top at dawn tomorrow — and we're going to lead the way!" he announced. "The high command has given us tremendous responsibility. We will take over Serre, and then defend and secure the left flank."

On the eve of the attack, St. John projected an air of confidence that spread throughout his platoon. In fact, his men seemed downright cheerful, singing and joking even though it was raining and the trenches oozed with a foot of mud and water.

"What should I come back with when we capture Serre?" private Harry Bloor, another teenage soldier, asked St. John. "A German helmet or an officer's wristwatch?"

"How about coming back with your life," said St. John.

Harry laughed. "You can count on that."

Despite his outward poise and coolness, the teenage lieutenant was too nervous to sleep. He was about to lead his men in their first big attack of the Great War. *Everyone says it's going to be an easy walkover*, he told himself. *But we are inexperienced. What if something goes wrong? No, don't think that way. The high command has placed great faith in me and my men. We just have to get to the trenches before the Germans — if there are any left — have time to set up their machine guns. But everyone says the Germans are already dead. There's nothing to worry about. I hope.*

At seven in the morning, St. John sloshed through the muddy trench, patting his men on the back, shaking their hands, wishing them good luck. He had to stay busy to hide the jitters. "Twenty minutes to go, boys," he announced.

His men were more subdued than they were the previous night. Some were still cracking jokes, but most were quiet. And most everyone was smoking.

At exactly 7:20 A.M., shrill whistles blew along the trench. Captain Riley shouted, "Over the top you go, boys!"

St. John was among the first to "jump the lid" (climb out of the trench) in the first wave of Accrington Pals. They passed through the gaps in their barbed wire and lay down in no-man's-land until all 180 men were in position. At 7:30 A.M., the British artillery barrage on the German front line stopped, the whistles blew, and St. John and his fellow Pals stood up. Then, as ordered, they began a steady march forward, five yards between each man, their rifles pointing up rather than toward the enemy trenches 250 yards away.

St. John wondered if the Pals, in their heavy packs, could reach the trenches before any German survivors had time to set up their machine guns. With each step, St. John's tense body began to relax. *No resistance so far. Keep walking.* He glanced to his left and to his right. *We're all in alignment. We're doing . . .*

A shot rang out. Then another and another. Suddenly, the entire no-man's-land erupted in machine gun fire from enemy lines. *No! This can't be! Their guns were supposed to have been destroyed!*

Despite what British military planners believed, the Germans' underground concrete bunkers had withstood the weeklong bombardment. Seeing the British troops advancing, the enemy responded quickly, manning hundreds of machine guns spaced three yards apart along their trenches. The Germans stared in disbelief at the slow, orderly pace of the British infantrymen who kept walking — not running — in long, straight lines toward them.

The sweeping machine guns mowed down the Pals like a scythe through wheat. Soldiers by the second fell to the turf dead. Many of them never had a chance to fire their weapons before they died. So many bullets flew through the air in the morning sun they reminded St. John of a big, glistening fan. Shells from the heavy guns at Serre burst all around the Pals. So did deafening, screeching whizbangs, aerial torpedoes, canister shells, and rifle grenades.

The horror-stricken teenager was at a loss. He wanted to drop, turn around, and low-crawl back to the safety of the British trenches. But he and the rest of the battalion had been trained to follow orders, and so he shouted to those still standing, "Keep marching! Advance!"

The proud Pals moved forward, first one wave, then another and another and another. *If I don't get shot, I'll probably get blown up,* St. John thought. Everywhere he looked, men were falling or writhing in pain in the weeds. The scene was too much for a 16-year-old — for anyone — to fully comprehend. Hundreds of shell holes opened up with nonstop explosions. In the smoke, he saw there no longer was a Pals line in the first wave. Only a few dozen men from his platoon were advancing; the rest were casualties. He turned around and saw the second wave moving forward but, as one man after another fell dead, that line soon melted away. So did the third and the fourth wave.

Only 50 yards from the enemy machine gunners, St. John and the few others in the first wave were stopped by the Germans' barbed wire. A week of British shelling hadn't destroyed all the barbed wire hidden in the long grass and weeds, forcing the surviving Pals to create their own paths using wire cutters.

In the mayhem, St. John heard a continuous hissing noise, like a railway engine letting off steam. The German machine guns were heating up, their barrels turning red.

A shell burst several yards away, knocking him down. The blast rang his ears and stars flitted across his vision. He scrambled to his feet and moved forward again. Seeing comrades dropping everywhere, he wondered how it was possible he hadn't been hit. And then he was.

Once through the barbed wire, about 20 yards from the

enemy line, he took a bullet in his right thigh and crashed to the ground. Blood gushed out. Fearing he would bleed to death, he took off his belt and tied it around the upper part of his leg. That's when he got shot again, this time in the right hand. The searing pain from the two wounds made him grimace. *I can't go any farther. I've got to turn back.* Then he saw a sight that angered and sickened him. The enemy was shooting at — and killing — the wounded Pals. *Those heartless Huns!*

He stared into the cold-blooded eyes of the closest German, whose machine gun was now aimed directly at him. *He's going to kill me!* St. John thought. But then the German shouted in anger and pounded on his weapon. *It's jammed! His gun is jammed! Here's my chance.* St. John rolled on his side and wiggled out of his pack. Then he crawled, pulled, and stumbled over the barbed wire in a desperate attempt to escape across no-man's-land. He gritted his teeth from the pain and felt increasingly woozy. *Don't lose consciousness.* His hand throbbed, his thigh felt on fire. He grew weaker. *Don't give up. Keep moving.*

Wherever he crawled, he was in within a few feet of a dead or dying comrade. Never in his young life had he imagined that he would witness such dreadful carnage.

St. John came across the body of a young soldier lying on his back, his ashen face frozen, his eyes locked in fear. Blood was still trickling out of his chest and neck. It took a moment before St. John recognized him — his 16-year-old buddy Horace Isles. *Oh, no! Not Horace. If only he had listened to his sister.*

Ever so slowly, St. John painfully crawled toward the British line. On the way, he spotted a teenage comrade, Jim Iley, working a machine gun. Jim had been shot, and his face was covered in blood. "Jim, leave the gun and come with me," St. John ordered.

"No, sir. I can't. There's no one to look after the gun, and I can't leave it."

"Godspeed, Jim." St. John started crawling when he heard a groan. He turned around and saw Jim slumped over the weapon.

Nearing the friendly side of the battlefield, St. John noticed the shelling and machine-gun fire had slackened considerably. Finally, he reached the top of the trench and was helped down. *I made it.* Then everything went black.

When St. John woke up, the British trenches were jammed with thousands of wounded like him. What few medics they had were overwhelmed and under-supplied.

He learned that only seven in the first wave of 180 Pals reached the German line. The rest were killed or wounded. Within 10 minutes of the British assault, the heart and soul of Accrington was virtually destroyed — 584 of the 720 Pals were dead, wounded, or missing. Nearly half of the 120,000 British soldiers who fought in the Battle of the Somme that day were casualties — 19,240 dead, 35,494 seriously wounded, and 2,152 missing. A few heroic British units managed to reach the enemy's trenches and storm the concrete blockhouses and fortified villages, but a German counterattack drove them out.

For Great Britain, it was the worst day in its modern military history.

St. John was one of the lucky ones. He survived and was transported to a hospital in England where he was treated for his wounds. During his recovery, a fellow teenage soldier, Harry Wilkinson, was in the bed next to him. Despite their losses, neither of them was depressed. Instead they talked about the glory and pride of their unit.

"We knew we were going to certain death, but not one man faltered," said Harry.

"Yes," agreed St. John, "it was a sad but proud moment."

"The Germans were pounding us with machine-gunfire, deadly shrapnel, and high-explosive shells. But we went on and on until we dropped. The line never wavered."

"That's because we never give up," St. John stressed, clenching his first. "We're Accrington Pals."

After a two-month recovery, St. John returned to France and rejoined the Eleventh Battalion. On the night of March 7, 1917, he was attending an officers' meeting at company headquarters near Puisieux-au-Mont when it took a direct hit from an enemy shell, killing or wounding them all. The explosion shattered St. John's left leg, and three weeks later it was amputated. During his eight-month recovery in a hospital in England, the War Office wanted to discharge him from the military. But the 17-year-old officer refused, claiming that once he got his artificial limb, he would be "quite fit in every other way" to serve his country until the end of the war. The military agreed and assigned him to a desk job in London. After the war, he followed in his father's footsteps and became a vicar at a church in Chittoe, Wiltshire, England.

During World War II, St. John served in the Royal Navy and became the chaplain to the Royal Marines at Chatham. After the war in 1945, he returned to his parish at Chittoe. He died in 1976, with a legacy as the youngest officer in modern British military history.

THE NAVY'S YOUNGEST HERO

CALVIN GRAHAM

World War II had been raging for eight months when Calvin Graham made up his mind that he was going to join the Navy. Never mind that he was only 12 years old. He was sure he could trick the veteran recruiting officer into letting him enlist.

Calvin was big for his age — five feet two inches and 122 pounds. And he was tough. Born in Canton, Texas, in 1930, to poor, sharecropping parents, Calvin started picking cotton when he was old enough to walk. He was eight when his father died. His mother remarried two years later, but his stepfather was an abusive drunk who threw him out of the house at the age of 10. Calvin moved in with his married sister and stayed with her until the summer of 1942 when he figured the navy could use a strapping, patriotic young — very young — man. He was stirred by the images he saw in newsreels of Japanese planes attacking and sinking American ships in Hawaii's Pearl Harbor on December 7, 1941.

On August 14, he and his friend Larry Jacobs, who was only 15, walked into the naval recruiting office in Houston, claiming they were 17. The underage boys filled out papers and took various tests. "Looks like you two would make good sailors," said the recruiter, handing each a form. "But without birth certificates, you'll need your parents' signatures verifying that you're seventeen. And, oh, the signatures on this form must have the seal of a notary — a person who can certify that the signatures are real."

When the boys left the office, Larry groaned, "What are we going to do? We can forge our moms' names, but how can we get our papers notarized?"

Calvin flashed a sly grin and said, "I know how. My brother Frank stayed at the Landmark Hotel for a while and used the manager's notary seal on this same kind of form when he forged my mother's signature and enlisted in the navy."

"How old is he?"

"Fourteen. He faked his way in. We can, too. The manager keeps a notary seal press in his desk drawer. We just need to borrow it for a few seconds without him catching us."

Later that day, Calvin walked into the rundown hotel and chatted with the manager. Larry called the manager from a pay phone across the street and, in an excited voice, reported, "I see smoke coming out of a window on the fourth floor of your hotel!" The manager charged out from behind his desk and ran up the stairs. Calvin opened the desk drawer, pulled out the seal press, applied the seal on both his and Larry's forms, returned the seal press, and fled. After exchanging the forms and signing the names of each other's mother, the boys went back to the recruiting office the next day and were sworn into the navy.

Calvin was 12 years, 4 months, and 12 days old.

"Do you believe it, Larry?" Calvin yelped, thrusting his fists in the air. "We're seamen! This is the happiest day of my life!"

He, Larry, and the other Texas recruits took a train to the naval training center in San Diego, California, for further testing and physicals. During Calvin's dental exam, the dentist said, "You're too young to be in the navy."

"I am not," Calvin objected. "I'm seventeen."

"You're lying, boy. Your twelve-year molars aren't even in yet. I don't know how you snookered the recruiter, but you need to go back home." He handed Calvin his file and said, "Take this over to the medical officer for discharge."

Fighting back tears, the boy shuffled off, lost in a fog of anger and crushing disappointment. *There must be a way*, he thought. When he saw the dentist turn his back, Calvin quietly but swiftly scurried over to the desk and slipped his file in the APPROVED stack. He remained in the navy.

Compared to the other trainees, the dimple-cheeked boy was the smallest in boot camp. No one questioned his age except Malcolm Burns, an 18-year-old trainee who kept needling him about his smooth face and childlike stature. "I think you're a little grade-school punk who's run away from home," Burns sneered. "You're not old enough to sprout a whisker."

Calvin socked him in the jaw. Malcolm retaliated with a flurry of punches that split Calvin's lip. But Calvin had made his point: Don't mess with him. If anyone wondered about his age, they never said it to his face.

After being rushed through boot camp in only a few weeks because of the war, Calvin became a gunnery mate on the new battleship USS *South Dakota*, which sailed for the South Pacific — an area dominated by the mighty Japanese navy.

When the ship was out of sight of land, Calvin felt elated. He had never been on the ocean before and was enthralled by the way the rippling royal blue waters melded with the pale blue sky. He inhaled the warm salt air and thought, *I can't believe I'm in the navy! This is a dream come true.*

Two days later, the ship rocked and rolled in a nasty storm that whipped up 30-foot waves. For hours on end, the vessel climbed a wave and then plunged into a trough while swaying side to side. Gripping a railing on the deck, Calvin stared down into the watery chasm and then up at a mountain of water over and over. Turning green and seasick, he threw up. He learned a valuable lesson: Never upchuck on the windward side, because it will blow back in your face. He felt so sick he wanted to die and lay on the cargo deck, thinking, *Combat can't be any worse than this.*

He soon found out for himself. On October 26, the *South Dakota* was part of a task force of other American vessels near the Santa Cruz Islands, about 1,000 miles east of Australia, when the ship's speaker came to life: "Battle stations! Battle stations!"

Calvin was so keyed up over facing his first combat that he tripped on the steps while scrambling topside. When he reached his post as second loader of the forecastle antiaircraft gun, he scanned the dark clouds, looking for enemy planes.

He soon heard a low droning noise that grew increasingly loud, like angry bees. Emerging from the clouds whirred dozens of Japanese fighter planes. "There they are!" he shouted in a voice that quaked from fear. More than 50 Japanese dive-bombers, torpedo planes, and Zeroes swooped down from all directions, attacking the *South Dakota* and other nearby ships, including the aircraft carrier *Enterprise*.

Working at a feverish pace, Calvin hustled to keep the three-barreled antiaircraft gun supplied with ammo as the gunner raked the skies. The din from the ship's weapons barely drowned out the roar of the enemy planes and American aircraft that had now intercepted them. Calvin glanced up every few seconds as the sky filled with puffs of smoke and burning trails of planes that were struck and falling.

Suddenly, he spotted a torpedo plane zooming low straight off the bow. To Calvin it looked like the pilot was aiming directly at him. The boy froze in terror when he saw a deadly torpedo drop from the plane. But the pilot had misjudged his target. To Calvin's relief, the torpedo whistled over the ship and dropped harmlessly into the sea.

Another enemy plane whizzed by from the stern but its torpedo also missed. As the aircraft flew over him, Calvin yelled to the gunner, "Let him have it!" A powerful stream of ack-ack — slang for antiaircraft fire — ripped into the left wing, snapping it off, and the plane plunged into the ocean. "Yes!" shouted Calvin.

But there was little time to celebrate. Seemingly appearing out of nowhere, more Japanese planes zipped, rolled, and dived into the ship's curtain of ack-ack. Whatever fright Calvin felt diminished with each enemy plane that blew up in the sky or spiraled into the water.

Unfortunately, one Japanese dive-bomber weaved through the Americans' heavy firepower and dropped its load on the bow of the *South Dakota.* The battleship shuddered, and the bow burst into a fireball. The force from the explosion picked up Calvin and slammed him against a bulkhead, nearly knocking the breath out of him.

He scrambled to his feet and returned to his post, feeding his gunner the ammo needed to try to prevent another direct hit. Occasionally, the boy glanced at fellow seamen who were removing the dead and dying from the smoldering bow. The fear that he thought was gone had returned with a vengeance. But he was too busy to deal with emotions. He and his crewmates now faced an even more desperate situation — a suicidal assault. The fighter planes from the *Enterprise* had crippled two Japanese aircraft carriers. As a result, the enemy pilots had no place to land, so they tried crashing their planes into American ships with devastating effect. The *Enterprise* and two destroyers were badly damaged while the aircraft carrier *Hornet* and another destroyer sank.

With all guns blazing, the *South Dakota* prevented any enemy plane from further damaging it. The battleship had knocked 26 Japanese aircraft out of the sky with Calvin's gun crew accounting for seven kills.

When he returned to his bunk, the boy was soaked in sweat. But he felt exhilarated over his first combat experience, and although he had felt scared, he was proud he never panicked. "Woo-eee," he crowed to his good buddy Red Hezil, 18. "I never had this much excitement in grade school back in Houston."

Red raised his eyebrows and said, "Grade school? Didn't you ever go to high school?"

"I, um, uh, meant high school."

Other slips of the tongue started raising suspicion about his age. As the ship steamed to the island of New Caledonia for repairs, his gunnery officer, Lieutenant Sargent Shriver, confronted Calvin. "Tell me straight, Seaman Graham. You're not anywhere close to seventeen, are you?"

Calvin shifted from one foot to the other, stalling for time. *Do I tell the truth? Should I lie?* Calvin cleared his throat. "The truth, sir, is I'm a little younger than seventeen."

Shriver furrowed his brows and asked, "Just how much younger? Fifteen?" When Calvin shook his head, the officer muttered, "My God, you're *fourteen*?"

Calvin lowered his eyes and mumbled, "Actually, sir, I'm . . ." He cringed. "I'm twelve. But I'll be thirteen in six months."

Shriver put his hands to his face and shook his head. "I don't believe this. A mere child fooled the U.S. Navy! Incredible!"

After Calvin confessed how he had lied and forged the papers, the boy pleaded with Shriver, "Please let me stay onboard, at least until the ship has completed its tour of duty. I know I'm young, but I've been trained as a seaman, and I do a good job as a second loader. Please?"

Calvin's pleading worked, and he was allowed to remain onboard.

Three weeks later, the *South Dakota* joined 19 ships in a new task force. Its mission: Intercept a large Japanese convoy and prevent the enemy from attacking Allied troops on the island of Guadalcanal. Whichever side controlled the island, located 750 miles northeast of Australia, would have the upper hand in the South Pacific.

At nightfall on November 14, the captain told his crew: "We are entering an action area with no great certainty what forces we'll encounter. We might be ambushed or face some sort of disaster. But whatever happens, I hope to bring all of you back alive. Good luck to all of us."

Calvin's heart was beating double-time, but he wasn't as terrified as he was during his first combat. At his battle station in the warm air, he gazed over the calm sea, which was lit by a silvery quarter moon. "It doesn't seem right to go and fight on such a pretty night," he told Red.

"When did you turn into a poet, in grade school?" Red cracked.

Before Calvin could retort, all gunners were ordered to load their weapons, which Calvin and his crew did in half the normal time. The ship's bells rang twice, signaling for the big guns to open fire on a Japanese destroyer that came into view. Blinding tongues of flame shot out of the main guns. Then the secondary guns opened up.

As the American destroyer *Preston* raced in to finish off the enemy vessel, more Japanese ships moved in and attacked. The *Preston* was pummeled and exploded in flames. Calvin, who felt the concussion from the blast, watched in horror as the *Preston* rolled over on her starboard side and slipped under the surface, claiming the lives of 117 men and her captain. Calvin was stunned at how fast the ship went down. *Could that happen to us?* he wondered.

An all-out sea battle was raging through the night. American vessels *Gwin* and *Walke* took major shelling, forcing their crews to abandon ship. The *South Dakota* was getting hit, too, but not as badly, and she maneuvered into a better position. Dead ahead Calvin saw the burning wreckage of the U.S. ships and dozens of sailors clinging to floating debris, waiting for rescue from nearby cruisers.

More shells struck the *South Dakota*. Calvin twitched with every impact. "Don't think about them," Red counseled. "Just focus on your job. It's all up to fate."

Crews were patching minor holes when the battleship lost electrical power. Everything went out — radar, fire control, turret motors, ammunition hoists, and radios. Even her guns locked up and couldn't move.

"This doesn't look good," Red told Calvin. "It's like we're blindfolded and handcuffed." It was worse than that. Japanese ships were surrounding the defenseless *South Dakota*.

"Graham! Get over here!" shouted Lieutenant Shriver. "Take this message to Lieutenant Smith. Hurry!"

Just as Calvin grabbed the note, someone yelled, "Down!" Calvin flopped behind a stack of heavy shells and curled up in a ball. A teeth-rattling, eardrum-shattering blast shook the ship and sent up a huge fireball. The force of the explosion shoved Calvin 10 feet through a doorway, and he tumbled down three floors of iron stairs. Bruised and battered, he staggered to his feet, not knowing where he was at first. When he finally got his bearings, he hustled up to the main deck, which was on fire. He found Lieutenant Smith and handed him the message.

"Good God, seaman, you're face is covered in blood," the officer told him. "Shrapnel is sticking out of your left cheek."

In an instant, Calvin became aware of the sharp pain in his jaw and mouth. He pulled out a small jagged piece of metal from his cheek. Then he took off his undershirt, wrapped it from under his chin to the top of his head, and tied it to stem the bleeding.

Another officer who was helping the wounded, shouted, "Graham, we need you on rescue duty!"

Despite the throbbing pain, Calvin began dragging unconscious and wounded sailors away from the fire. Near his antiaircraft gun, Calvin found a body. He flipped it over and gasped. "Nooo!" Calvin wailed. He burst into sobs. It was his good buddy Red Hezil. *This could have been me*, he thought. *If*

I hadn't been ordered to carry the message, I would have been right next to Red.

"Graham! Over here!" shouted a gunnery mate.

Calvin wiped away his tears and dashed over to help carry a seaman whose legs had been blown off in the blast. Staying busy kept his mind off of losing Red.

When partial power was restored to the ship, Calvin returned to his battle station. The *South Dakota*'s guns blasted at the enemy, which was closing in fast. The Japanese launched a flurry of torpedoes at the ship, but all of them missed. However, a steady stream of shells continued to smash into her. Although most failed to penetrate her armor plate or explode, 42 landed on her superstructure, cutting the ship's communications cables, shattering her radar, and disabling several guns.

Fires sprang up everywhere, including one that had trapped several officers. Calvin and fellow sailors rushed to their rescue, dousing the blaze and saving the men.

Other ships, including the battleship *Washington*, destroyed or drove off the remaining Japanese vessels. Meanwhile, the damaged *South Dakota* withdrew from combat, having suffered a toll of 39 crewmen dead and 56 wounded.

With the flames snuffed out onboard and the wounded receiving emergency treatment, Calvin returned to his bunk and collapsed. His slender body began to shake uncontrollably from the pain and weariness he felt and the death and destruction he witnessed. *I hope I never have to go through this again*, he thought.

Over the course of the battle, which lasted three days, the Americans lost 9 ships, 36 planes, and 1,732 men while destroying 17 Japanese vessels, including 11 troop ships. The enemy also lost 64 aircraft and 1,900 men. It proved to be a pivotal moment in the war in the South Pacific, turning the tide in the Americans' favor.

The *South Dakota* chugged to New Caledonia for emergency repairs and then sailed halfway around the world to the Brooklyn Navy Yard for an overhaul.

In New York, a ceremony was held to honor crewmen who went above and beyond the call of duty. For his brave actions during combat, Calvin was awarded the Bronze Star, the Purple Heart, and the Navy Unit Commendation Medal. As he presented the medals to Calvin, the ship's commander, Captain Thomas Gatch, whispered to him, "If you can get your mother's permission, I'll see what I can do about keeping you in the navy."

Calvin beamed. "Thank you, sir!"

While on leave, Calvin returned home and, after an impassioned plea, convinced his mom to give her consent. He returned to duty with high hopes that he would remain in the navy. But Captain Gatch had been transferred, and the acting captain made it clear that he didn't want a 12-year-old aboard his ship.

Before the issue could be resolved, Calvin's grandmother died. The acting captain gave him a pass to attend her funeral in Houston and ordered him to report to the nearest recruiting office and reveal his true age.

After the funeral, Calvin followed orders and confessed to the recruiters that he had lied about his age. Rather than give him an honorable discharge, an outraged navy official ordered Calvin thrown in the brig (navy jail) and stripped of his medals. The boy's family and his fellow seamen had no clue he had been locked up.

He remained imprisoned for three months until a fellow prisoner who was released from the brig contacted Calvin's sister. When she learned what the navy had done to her little brother, she demanded his immediate release. "Either you free Calvin right away," she told an official, "or I'll contact the newspapers and tell them that the cold-hearted navy has been holding a 12-year-old boy in the brig for months."

The navy gave in. In April 1943 — just days after he turned 13 — Calvin was released from the brig and kicked out of the service without an honorable discharge or access to veterans' benefits.

Despite the cruel treatment, Calvin didn't complain. In his hometown, he was treated as a hero and attended several American Legion bond rallies to raise money for the war effort. At one rally, he told the crowd, "I came out of the navy twenty-two pounds heavier. I'm strong and healthy and I learned that we must do whatever we can — even give our lives — to protect America. I'm not allowed to fight anymore, but I guarantee you that the day I turn seventeen, I'm enlisting."

True to his word, Calvin enlisted in the U.S. Marine Corps at 17. He remained in the corps for three years until he fell from a pier while on duty and broke his back, ending his military career and leaving him permanently disabled.

Although serving in the U.S. Marines qualified him as a veteran, he wrote to congressmen pleading to have his navy record restored and his medals returned. In 1978 — 36 years after he served on the South Dakota *— his efforts paid off and he was given an honorable discharge and all his medals, except the Purple Heart (which is awarded to servicemen who suffered combat wounds).*

Calvin died at his home in Fort Worth, Texas, in 1992 at the age of 62. Eighteen months later, Secretary of the Navy John Dalton presented Calvin's widow, Mary, with the Purple Heart that had been denied him for all those years.

Military historians believe that Calvin Graham was the youngest U.S. serviceman to serve in World War II.

THE ONE-MAN ARMY

★

JAMES L. (JIM) DAY

Being scared wasn't an option for Jim Day — not if he wanted to live.

Hour after hour, day after day, the brave teenager single-handedly defended a key position from an unrelenting swarm of Japanese soldiers. Scurrying from side to side in a muddy hilltop bomb crater on the South Pacific island of Okinawa, Jim blasted away with his rifle and machine gun and hurled grenades to keep the determined enemy at bay. All Jim's comrades were dead, dying, or too sick to help. Bleary-eyed from lack of sleep, bleeding from shrapnel wounds, and exhausted from three horrifying days and nights of fighting, the gritty young corporal refused to give up.

Shortly after midnight on the fourth day of his courageous stand, the Japanese launched yet another assault on his position, opening up with a barrage of mortar rounds. Rattled by thunderous explosions that showered him with bloodstained mud, Jim dodged the incoming shells and then let loose with his own firepower that mowed down the latest dedicated squad of Japanese who tried — and failed — to kill him.

When silence returned to the hill, the dog-tired teen — caked in dried muck and blood — leaned against the side of the crater to catch his breath. *Maybe I shouldn't have quit school after all*, he thought.

In 1943, Jim dropped out of Ritenour High School in Overland, Missouri, near Saint Louis. Swayed by a patriotic desire to fight in World War II, he enlisted in the U.S. Marines at 17 and breezed through boot camp.

Sent to fight in the South Pacific, Jim proved such a natural soldier that he was promoted to corporal and became a squad leader in Weapons Company of the Second Battalion, Twenty-second Marine Regiment, Sixth Marine Division. Months of combat in the Marshall Islands and Guam had forged in him a strong battle-tested confidence. He was fully prepared when the marines launched a bloody invasion of the Japanese-held island of Okinawa in 1945.

Jim and his comrades were warned it would be a deadly, ferocious conflict unlike anything they had ever experienced. "The Japs know that if they can't hold Okinawa, they lose," battalion commander Lieutenant Colonel Horatio Woodhouse told his men. "The Japs have a word for an all-or-nothing situation upon which everything else depends — *tenozan*. This word applies to their defense of Okinawa. They will not surrender. They will fight to the death."

The key to breaking the enemy's stronghold was for the marines to secure a certain valley surrounded by three hills, including one shaped like a loaf of bread that they called Sugar Loaf. For almost a week, marines charged into the valley in front of Sugar Loaf, only to die or be driven back under intense artillery, mortar, and machine-gun fire.

On May 14, Jim and his buddy Private First Class Dale Bertoli volunteered to reinforce F Company, a small unit under siege on Sugar Loaf. Although they were still only teenagers, the two friends were savvy soldiers and expert marksmen who deftly handled a variety of weapons.

Jim led four men up the western side of Sugar Loaf and found that most of the marines from F Company were dead or dying, including its lieutenant who, in weakening gasps, told Jim, "Take whoever . . . can fight . . . and capture . . . the right slope." Then the lieutenant wheezed and died.

Turning to Dale, Jim said, "If we can secure the slope and disrupt the Japs' crossfire, our guys should be able to advance. At the least, we can halt the Japs from counterattacking our line, because they'd have to come across us."

"Lead the way, Corporal!" Dale said with his typical enthusiasm.

Jim and his squad, which now numbered eight, bravely

fought their way up the hill under a barrage of heavy artillery and machine-gun fire. When they reached the top of the western slope, they dropped into a 30-foot-wide bomb crater and set up positions. Almost immediately, the Japanese began attacking them.

"Incoming!" Dale shouted, diving into the mud for cover. Mortar rounds burst in thunderous, head-pounding explosions, killing three marines and seriously wounded three others.

"Medic!" shouted Dale, who along with Jim wasn't hurt. "We need a medic up here!"

Sergeant Narolian West and two other unarmed corpsmen reached the crater to treat and retrieve the wounded. Within seconds, they all came under attack by 20 yelling Japanese soldiers who tried to storm the position. With weapons from their dead and wounded comrades by their side, Jim and Dale fired furiously at the enemy.

"They're like rats in a feeding frenzy!" Dale yelled.

Jim kept swiveling as he blazed away, killing one to his left, one in front, and another to his right. Just then he heard West shout, "Behind you!"

Jim whirled around and saw three enemy soldiers leaping into the crater next to the medics who were still treating the wounded. "Duck!" he ordered the corpsmen. Then he fired his automatic weapon from the hip, cutting down the three Japanese with deadly accuracy. As each enemy soldier clutched his fatal wound, he fell on top of a corpsman. Jim then dashed to the back of the crater and heaved four grenades, wiping out an entire squad. Not wasting a second, he raced to the opposite side and joined Dale in killing the remaining invaders.

"We did it," said Dale, huffing and puffing. "I don't see any more Japs."

"Yeah, but they'll be back."

West went over to Jim and shook his hand. "Thanks, Corporal. You saved our lives." Pointing to the three wounded marines, West said, "They're in real bad shape. We're taking them off the hill."

After the corpsmen left with the wounded, Dale asked Jim, "Do you think we can defend this position?"

"I think so. We have F Company on the other side of the crest." Noticing that his pal seemed pale and shaky, Jim asked, "Are you feeling okay?"

"I'm kind of achy and my stomach is upset. I might have picked up a bug, but I'll be fine."

"You don't look so good, Dale."

"Yeah, well, you ain't exactly Hollywood handsome, either."

During the night, the two heard the soldiers from F Company wage a ferocious, close-in battle with the enemy. From the shouts, orders, and anguished cries, it was obvious to the teenagers, who couldn't see their comrades, that their fellow marines were losing lives and the fight.

"They're in trouble," said Jim. He and Dale shot and tossed grenades at every shadow that moved in the direction of F Company. Soon the two soldiers heard the sounds of the surviving marines being evacuated down the hill. Jim and Dale were now the only Americans left on Sugar Loaf.

"What do you think now?" Dale asked.

"Hundreds of Japs against two Americans? I'd say the odds are definitely in our favor," Jim declared with a wink. "We should stay put rather than withdraw. The hill is swarming with Japs. We know how to use our weapons and we're great shots. If we leave this hill undefended, then there's no way the marines can get across the valley."

"We don't have a radio or field phone to communicate with headquarters. No one knows we're here, and we don't know what our battalion is planning next."

"We can't worry about a half hour into the future let alone about what's going on elsewhere. Our job is to stay here and take out the enemy."

"Our job is to survive," added Dale, now shivering and feverish from his illness.

"Shhh," whispered Jim. "I hear rocks sliding down the hill." That could only mean one thing. The enemy was climbing up. "Here they come again!"

A Japanese squad of 10 that split into two units attacked from opposite sides, forcing Jim and Dale to fight with their backs against each other. Four enemy soldiers jumped into the crater, but the two marines killed them.

Twice more during the night, the enemy sent squads to attack the lone American outpost. The gutsy teenagers successfully fought off the assaults by throwing hand grenades and firing their weapons while moving constantly so the flashes from their guns wouldn't give away their exact locations. Neither marine got any sleep.

Shortly before dawn, Jim announced, "We're running low on ammo."

"We have another problem, Jim. I'm really sick. I'm burning up, getting weaker by the minute, and I have diarrhea."

"Okay, stay here. I'll try to find ammo and some medical supplies." Jim left the crater and went partway down the hill. He came across two amtracs — armored tracked landing vehicles — that earlier had tried to deliver critical supplies to F Company but had been knocked out. Jim raided the disabled vehicles for grenades, bullets, and rations. But there was no medicine to treat Dale.

At daylight on May 15, the Japanese pounded Sugar Loaf with mortars and then crept up the slope. Once again, Jim and Dale fired back.

"Ah, damn it! I've been hit!" Jim cried out in anguish. Shrapnel from an exploding shell had sliced across both arms. Fortunately, the hot metal hadn't severed any veins or arteries or broken any bones. He wrapped each arm to stop the bleeding. Then he jammed fresh clips into his rifle and fired away. Glancing to his right, he noticed Dale had trouble holding on to his weapon. Instead, he was hurling grenades that bounced down the hill, exploding in front of the advancing enemy.

When the attack was beaten back, Jim turned to congratulate Dale and saw that his buddy was slumped over. He raced over to him. "What's wrong?"

Holding up a bloody hand, Dale moaned, "I took a bullet here and in my leg."

After bandaging Dale's wounds, Jim felt his comrade's forehead. "You have a high fever."

"My joints and muscles are hurting so bad I can't even hold up my weapon," Dale complained. "And look at this." He ripped open his shirt, revealing a nasty red rash on his chest.

Jim let out a whistle. "You have all the signs of dengue fever." The tropical disease, which is transmitted by mosquitoes, can leave victims disabled and in pain for up to a week. "Drink lots of water, so you don't dehydrate."

Later that morning, the two watched their fellow marines attempt to assault Sugar Loaf and oust the Japanese. But their comrades were fully exposed to raking fire from nearby hills and suffered heavy casualties. With Dale unable to shoot anymore, Jim did all he could, firing into a column of Japanese running toward Sugar Loaf.

He soon heard a marine from nearby moaning for a medic. "I'm going to check it out," he told Dale.

"Be careful. It could be a trap. One of those Japs might know English and pretend he's a marine."

Jim slipped out of the crater and immediately drew fire from another ridge. He crawled about 40 yards and found four wounded marines pinned down in a shell hole. One by one, he carried them to the relative safety of the crater and helped bandage their wounds. Then he went back for their machine gun and ammunition. Although two of the men were in serious condition and defenseless, two others could at least shoot, so he had one of them guard the rear.

The other marine, Bob McDonald, was an expert at using a .30-caliber, air-cooled machine gun. Although he suffered a bad leg injury, he was able to set up his weapon on the forward wall of the crater and then mow down a Japanese squad that earlier had chased the retreating marines.

Soon, intense cannon fire from an antitank gun pummeled the crater. One shot scored a direct hit on the machine gun, pitching Jim up and backward. He landed hard in the mud, knocking the wind out of him and leaving him in pain. His hands and groin were bleeding from shrapnel wounds. When he got to his feet, he saw the machine gun was now a twisted piece of smoking metal. McDonald lay next to it. He was dead.

Before Jim could say anything, a salvo of mortar rounds slammed and exploded at the rear of the crater. One look made Jim wince. The other three marines he had rescued had been blown to bits.

Dale was on his knees, shaking, weak, and burning hot from dengue fever.

"There's no doubt about it," said Jim. "You need to be evacuated."

"Are you nuts?" Dale grumbled. "I'm not leaving you alone. I might not be able to use my hands to fire a weapon, but I can carry ammo for you. I can act as a lookout. No siree, I'm not letting you get all the glory," he joked. "We've gone through too much together."

That night seemed endless to the teenagers as the enemy launched a series of raids on the lonely outpost. Hearing the Japanese scramble up the rocks, Jim greeted them with a flurry of grenades. Those who survived his mini-barrage were backlit by flares that he fired, making it easy for Jim to shoot them as they neared the crest.

But by now, Dale was simply too weak to fight.

"Sorry, buddy," said Dale. "I just can't fight anymore."

"Let me take you back down."

"No. I've got to stay. I can be your lookout. You haven't slept in forty-eight hours."

"Neither have you."

"Get some shut-eye. I'll stand watch."

Just as Jim closed his eyes, two enemy soldiers jumped into the crater, but Jim grabbed his weapon and shot them. Then he raced to the edge and sprayed the area with bullets, driving the rest off. He felt lousy and tired and wet from a steady rain. The stench from the dead bodies in and around the crater only added to his misery.

The next day, marine tanks, artillery, and mortars pounded the nearby ridge where the Japanese had their greatest firepower. But the enemy was dug in too deep. From his vantage point, Jim watched in gloom as the valley turned into a bloody killing zone where whole squads and platoons of marines were wiped out.

When the clouds parted, his view became more alarming. Steady columns of Japanese reinforcements streamed toward the contested valley. Jim kept firing at them from 500 yards away, maintaining a lone but persistent thorn in the Japanese defenses.

Shortly after midnight May 17 — the beginning of the fourth day of his stand — Jim's rifle fire attracted considerable attention from prowling squads of Japanese raiders. All he could do was keep tossing grenades and shooting his weapon. Then mortar fire erupted.

"I think it's friendly fire," Jim said. "Our guys are trying to help us."

"Yeah, but it's getting a little too close for comfort," said Dale.

Unexpectedly, several shells landed inside the crater. The blasts unleashed a dangerous spray of white hot phosphorous, scorching Jim's legs and Dale's arms. Shrapnel ripped into them, too. They couldn't stop the shelling because they didn't have a radio.

At dawn, a runner from the Twenty-ninth Marines scrambled up to the crater. "You're ordered to get out right now." The division was about to start a massive bombardment by air, naval gunfire, and artillery and saturate the ridge in preparation of a fresh assault.

"Fine with me," said Jim. Exhausted from his nonstop defense of the outpost, reeking from filthy clothes and sweat, and partially deafened by enemy explosions, Jim helped carry his ill comrade down the hill.

Arriving at headquarters, Jim underwent an intense series of debriefings by staff officers. He described what he had seen from his observation post, including where the enemy had hidden machine-gun nests and bunkers. The vital information helped the marines pinpoint their targets.

While a thunderous American bombardment shelled Sugar Loaf, Jim washed up, ate a warm meal, and fell into a deep sleep. Dale, delirious from pain and fever, was carried off to a field hospital.

When Jim woke up, a fellow marine told him, "We've secured Sugar Loaf. Great job, Jim. Someone went there and counted all the dead Japs around your crater. He added up one hundred fifty-eight bodies, including twelve inside the hole."

Jim shook his head in disbelief. "They just kept coming and coming."

Two days after the hill was taken, Jim was called into the tent of battalion commander Horatio Woodhouse. "I'm recommending you for the Medal of Honor, son," said Woodhouse. "You gave no ground to the enemy, and your unwavering devotion to duty and valiant spirit contributed greatly in capturing Sugar Loaf."

"Thank you, sir," said the extremely humbled teenager. "I was just doing what I was trained to do — fight as a proud member of the U.S. Marine Corps."

The battle for Okinawa was the last major combat of World War II. It was also the bloodiest battle of the Pacific campaign, costing the lives of 12,000 Americans. Jim Day's courageous defense of his position on Sugar Loaf Hill helped his battalion to advance and crush the enemy's line across the island.

Dale Bertoli recovered from dengue fever and was back on the front lines within two weeks. Tragically, he was shot in the neck during a fierce firefight and died four days later.

Horatio Woodhouse was killed two days after his meeting with Jim, so the paperwork for the Medal of Honor was never sent, and Jim never pursued the matter.

After the war, Jim returned to Overland, Missouri, and earned his high school diploma from Ritenour. Then he reenlisted in the marines where he had a distinguished military career. As an officer, he fought in the Korean War and then served two tours of duty in the Vietnam War. He is believed to be the only marine to have been wounded and decorated for valor in all three wars. Among his many medals, he earned six Purple Hearts for combat injuries.

After a series of promotions, he became a major general in 1984 and was in charge of the marine base in, ironically, Okinawa. He retired two years later.

Although the paperwork for Jim's Medal of Honor recommendation was lost in the chaos of battle, a faded carbon copy was discovered in 1980 by a retired marine who was going through his World War II memorabilia. It took another 18 years for the paperwork to reach the appropriate officials.

On January 20, 1998 — more than half a century after his solitary, valiant actions as a teenage marine on Sugar Loaf Hill — Major General James L. Day was awarded the Medal of Honor. Nine months later, he died of a heart attack at age 73.

THE SABOTEUR

★

OTIS H. (KARL) KING

Surrendered, yes! Defeated, no!

Teenager Karl King silently repeated the motto of the Fourth Marine Regiment while marching daily with hundreds of other American prisoners of war from their rickety barracks to their slave-labor job at the grimy, bustling Mitsubishi Shipyards in Yokohama, Japan.

Surrendered, yes. Defeated, no!

He drummed those words in his head to stay strong, to stay steadfast, to stay alive. He and his fellow POWs lived a miserable, degrading life. They were housed in a cramped, freezing warehouse infested with rats, lice, and fleas, given a meager diet unfit for a dog, marched five miles round-trip every day to work 10 hours in the shipyards, and beaten and humiliated constantly.

But Karl was still an American, still a marine, and still a foe of the Japanese. Every day was a new opportunity to fight back against his enemies throughout his lengthy captivity in World War II. The youngest soldier in the Fourth Regiment had no guns, no ammo. But he knew how to inflict pain on the Japanese war effort in small, subtle ways with the only weapon he did have — sabotage.

Surrendered, yes. Defeated, no!

The beanpole of a kid from Texas could never have imagined that he would end up toiling under the cold eyes of vicious guards. No, he had pictured a long and adventurous military career the day he enlisted in the U.S. Marines in 1939, using a fake document that listed his age as 18 when, in fact, he was only 14.

His cash-strapped mother was fine with the lie, thinking the military would provide for Karl much better than she could. She believed he would make a good soldier because he excelled in ROTC, a student cadet program at Adamson High School in Dallas, before he dropped out. She wasn't too concerned about his safety because although war had erupted in Europe, the United States wasn't involved at the time.

Her skinny five-foot-ten son almost failed the physical because he was two pounds shy of the minimum weight. "Go to the grocery store and buy a pound of bananas," the sergeant told him. "Eat all of them and drink lots of water and then come back here to be weighed again."

Karl did as he was told and managed to meet the weight standard with an ounce to spare. A week before his fifteenth birthday, he was sworn in as a marine. By the time he had completed his training and was eventually shipped to the Fourth Regiment in the Philippines, Karl had grown to six-foot-one and weighed nearly 200 pounds.

He was stationed at Bataan, a Philippine peninsula across the bay from the capital of Manila, when the Japanese bombed Pearl Harbor. The following month, Japan attacked the Philippines. Terribly outnumbered and stuck with outdated weapons, the American and Filipino soldiers were under siege. Somehow, though, they held off the enemy for nearly six months, allowing the U.S. military crucial time to recover from the sneak attack on Pearl Harbor. The courageous stand in the Philippines would become known as the Alamo of the Pacific.

For the teenage private first class (PFC) it was baptism under fire, and he quickly learned the ways of jungle combat. During one patrol, enemy machine-gun fire kept Karl and his fellow marines pinned down, so he crawled to a nearby tree and lobbed a grenade into the machine-gun nest. To Karl's disbelief, the gunner threw it back. Karl dived for cover, but fortunately the grenade didn't explode.

It's a dud, he thought. On one hand, he was relieved. On the other, he was upset. *Another old grenade. Everything we have to fight with is old.* Figuring the firing pin had failed to ignite the fuse, Karl pulled out another old grenade and banged it against the stock of his rifle to drive home the firing pin. Then he hurled it. The enemy gunner picked up the grenade, but this time it blew up before he could throw it back.

The marine patrol advanced until the men engaged in another deadly firefight with the enemy. Unexpectedly, two Japanese soldiers, one behind the other, stepped out of the brush with their hands up. "They're surrendering!" Karl shouted. When four marines moved forward to take them prisoner, the first Japanese soldier threw himself belly-first on the ground while the second one manned a machine gun that was strapped to the first man's back. Stunned by the dirty trick, Karl took several seconds before he could react and shoot them. But by then, two marines were dead and the other two were wounded.

During another patrol, Karl and his comrades were harassed by snipers camouflaged in green uniforms and facial paint. The Japanese had tied themselves to tree limbs and were picking off marines one at a time. Just by chance, in the growing dusk, Karl saw a faint muzzle flash high in a banyan tree, but he couldn't see the sniper. Keeping his eyes on the tree, Karl braced his rifle on a fallen log and waited for another flash. When the sniper shot again, Karl opened fire. An enemy rifle tumbled to the ground, followed by the sniper, whose lifeless body, which was still tied to a rope, fell partway and begin swinging like the pendulum on a grandfather clock.

In April, the Japanese riddled Bataan with heavy bombing and artillery and then launched a major invasion. The marines stubbornly resisted, inflicting heavy losses on the attackers for six days until the outmanned defenders were forced to retreat.

"It's futile to keep fighting," an officer shouted to Karl and his squad. "Time to blow up our ammo dumps and warehouses, so the Japs can't use them. If you find a truck or jeep, drive it off the cliff. We don't want them to fall into enemy hands."

"Where should we go?" Karl asked.

"Hide in the jungle or find your own way to Corregidor. Just don't get captured!"

Karl turned to his best friend, 19-year-old Private First Class Isaac "Ike" Williams, a fellow Texan, and pointed to the tiny island of Corregidor, two and a half miles away. "Are you up for a swim?"

"Sure, I'm willin' to take my chances with the sharks," drawled Ike. "Bataan ain't no place to stay."

They rushed to the beach where they found a log large enough to support their packs and rifles. Then they jumped into the shark-infested waters and began pushing the log as they floated behind it, kicking furiously toward Corregidor as night fell.

They were among 2,000 who fled for their lives on boats, logs, or floating debris, or by swimming. When Karl glanced back at the explosions and fire on Bataan, the peninsula reminded him of an erupting volcano.

Karl and Ike reached Corregidor about an hour before dawn. Standing in the darkness in neck-deep water, they were confronted by marines who were guarding the rocky beach.

"Halt!" one of the guards challenged.

"Don't shoot! We're from the Fourth Regiment escaping from Bataan," Karl said.

"How do we know you're not Jap infiltrators?"

Without missing a beat, Ike burst into song, singing the new hit tune at the time, "The Yellow Rose of Texas." When he finished, he bellowed, "Boys, we're marines, we're from Texas, we're tired, and we're wet." The guards helped them out of the water and led them to their command post where they joined Company L, Third Battalion, Fourth Regiment. The following day, Karl and Ike removed a .50 caliber machine gun from a disabled military seaplane and took a position atop a 60-foot seaside cliff.

After the fall of Bataan, the Japanese aimed their heavy artillery at Corregidor. For 27 days, bombing runs and artillery fire blasted the tiny island from dawn to dusk, reducing most of it to rubble. The Americans held out as long as they could, but finally on May 7 . . .

"We're surrendering," an officer told Karl and Ike. "Pass the word."

The news staggered Karl. "I don't believe it!"

"Believe it, son. It's over. The brass [army officials] are already meeting with the Japs to end this bloodbath."

Ike wiped the tears that had welled up and grabbed Karl's arm. "Come on. It's time to put Plan B into motion."

They ran to their gun pit and unearthed a crate of hand grenades, a case of canned tomatoes, and a box of ammo that they had stashed. They planned to take a small boat they had hidden earlier in a beachside cave for just such an emergency. While they were putting their supplies together, Ike yelled, "What the hell!" Leaning out of the gun pit, he shouted to three men on the beach below, "Hey, you jerks! That's our boat!"

Ignoring him, the men pushed the boat out into the water and began paddling. They got about 100 yards before a Japanese patrol shot it so full of holes it sank, forcing the men to swim back to shore where they were captured.

With their escape boat gone, Karl and Ike were resigned to their fate. They sat on the edge of the gun pit and aimlessly tossed their hand grenades out into the bay. Then they dismantled their machine gun and rifles and threw the parts into the water. Neither said a word until Ike started singing, "I'll Never Smile Again."

The two returned to their company where they were told to bed down and wait for the Japanese. The next morning, the enemy soldiers rounded up the marines and searched them. Karl was forced to turn over his wristwatch to a soldier who already had six watches on his arm.

On May 23, the captors herded the prisoners aboard a rusty freighter that transported them across the bay to Manila. There, the POWs were paraded along Dewey Boulevard as trophies of war and as a demonstration of Japanese military power to the Filipinos who watched the march in somber silence. The Americans were kept in a prison camp for months before they were transferred to a slave-labor camp in Yokohama, Japan, where they would be forced to build warships in the Mitsubishi Shipyards. They arrived on Thanksgiving Day, 1942.

An icy fog from Tokyo Bay rolled in, slicing through the thin khaki clothes that now sagged on Karl's once robust body. The cold chill and the sight of his new home — a dismal gray warehouse — gave him the shivers. Inside were wooden platforms with three-by-six-foot grass mats for sleeping. Cracks in the walls and broken windows allowed the cold air to rush in. Each POW was given a number. Karl's was 960; Ike's, 961.

"You are numbered in groups of ten," an English-speaking Japanese official told the captives. "If one in your group of ten escapes, the other nine will be executed. If you do not do what you are told, you will be punished severely. You surrendered rather than died an honorable death in battle. You have disgraced yourself and your family. After Japan wins the war and you return home, you will have to wear a basket over your head so your parents will not be shamed by seeing your face. Our honorable emperor has spared your lives, so in return you will work gladly and diligently here in the shipyards for him."

Ike whispered to Karl, "They think we're cowards and unworthy of their respect. What they don't understand is that we choose to live so we can fight 'em again. They'll never suspect what we're about to do to 'em."

A few days after the prisoners began work at the shipyard, a submarine-chasing vessel that they had been forced to repair sank at the dock overnight. Karl learned that one of the POWs had secretly opened a valve that allowed seawater into the bilges, causing the ship to settle to the bottom.

For this sabotage, the Americans expected to be tortured or even executed as prime suspects. The *kempei tai* — the Japanese military police — swarmed over the yard, halting work and grilling the civilian workers. But believing the POWs were incapable of sabotage because they were so thankful to be alive, the police never questioned any of them.

On board the sunken vessel were crates of electrical motors for delivery to other ships at sea. The waterlogged engines were retrieved, dismantled, cleaned, and reassembled in the electric shop where Karl and Ike worked. After the motors were given a final test by civilian workers, the two POWs loaded them onto a truck. When no one was watching, Karl reached through an opening in the housing of each motor and yanked a wire free. The damage — made to look like the wire came loose or wasn't installed properly — would not be discovered until each engine reached its final destination.

One of Karl's jobs was to drive an electric-powered cart to a warehouse and pick up large reels of electrical cable for use in running power and communications in ships under construction. At the warehouse, Karl loaded three reels that the foreman had ordered, but then the teenage POW had an idea: *Why don't I take three more and then get rid of them? The Japs in the warehouse don't pay any attention to me. If I'm caught, I'm dead meat. But hey, it's worth the risk.* Although it was winter, he was sweating as he drove the cart out of the warehouse and to a remote part of the dock. Hiding behind a large shipping container, he shoved three reels into the bay. From then on, every time Karl went to the warehouse, he took extra cargo and dumped it into the water. He ended up getting rid of more than 100 reels — an act that delayed the completion of several ships because they ran out of cable.

One time, Ike was allowed to go with Karl to pick up the reels. On their return, Karl noticed an unguarded warehouse. While Ike acted as a lookout, Karl sneaked inside and found wooden crates of equipment that were slated to be installed in the control rooms of ships under construction.

Not knowing if he'd get another opportunity like this, Karl pulled out a makeshift cigarette lighter. Inside a small tin box were a piece of steel, a flint rock, and a strip of cloth. He struck the flint against the steel, creating a spark that lit the cloth. Then he ignited pieces of litter and shoved them into several crates until they caught on fire.

He raced out of the building, hopped on the cart, and left the scene with Ike. By the time they returned to the electric shop, the fire alarm sounded. Guards ordered POWs to rush to the warehouse, which was now fully engulfed in flames, and help fight the fire by forming a bucket brigade from the dock to the burning building.

"What a lovely sight this is, you firebug," Ike whispered to Karl.

Each POW in the bucket brigade "accidentally" spilled water as it was passed down the line on the way to the flames, so not much water reached the fire. The building and all its contents couldn't be saved.

A few days later, Karl and Ike were loading crates into a boxcar when they noticed the labels were in English: DELICATE ELECTRONIC INSTRUMENTS. HANDLE WITH CARE.

"Make sure no one is looking," Ike told Karl. Then Ike raised the crate and dropped it on the ground. "Oops," he said. He

picked it up and dropped it again. "Oops, how clumsy of me."
He did this with every crate before loading it onto the train.

The POWs were reminded often about the consequences of
getting caught for "accidentally" making a serious "mistake." A
foreman spotted a marine named Sparks cutting several critical
ship-bound cables too short, rendering them useless. The
foreman was especially angry because it was the last piece of
that particular cable anywhere in the shipyard. When the
"mistake" was discovered, the foreman screamed at Sparks,
grabbed a two-by-four chunk of wood, and savagely beat him.
Karl and Ike watched in anguish, powerless to help their fellow
American.

In Yokohama, Karl had fallen from his prewar weight of 200
pounds down to 118 because he, like the other POWs, wasn't
given enough to eat. They had to steal food whenever they had
the chance, so they carried cloth sacks tucked inside their belts
to hold any edible item they could swipe in the shipyard. Karl
looked forward to loading supplies onto freight trains bound
for Japanese army bases because it was his best opportunity for
thievery.

One of Karl's and Ike's favorite tricks was to tear a small hole
in the corner of a burlap bag of rice on top of a stack. By standing
next to the bag with their little cloth sacks open, the two took
turns catching the stream of grain flowing out of the torn bag.
They often collected as much as a pound of rice. Thanks to the
extra food he stole, Karl gained about 25 pounds.

But it wasn't without risk. One time, a guard uncovered
Karl's hidden stash of stolen rice during a search. As punishment,

Karl was tied to a post and ordered to spread his arms out to the side. Under each arm, the guard placed a sharpened bamboo pole with the point touching the underside of the forearm. Then he gave Karl a two-pound bucket of sand to grip in each hand.

Holding his arms out for any length of time was strenuous enough, but it was agony with the buckets of sand. Karl toughed it out as long as he could. Eventually, though, his arms began to sag under the weight of the sand until the point of each bamboo stake pierced the skin.

Don't show pain or cry out in agony, he told himself. He knew that to whimper, grunt, or groan would delight the enemy and prolong the agony. *Give no expression, show no emotion, and hope that this punishment will end soon.* He had to deny them the pleasure of his torment. His skinny arms dipped lower, forcing the razor-sharp bamboo further into his trembling muscles as falling droplets of blood turned the ground crimson. Outwardly, his face remained blank. But he was in misery. *I don't know how much more I can stand. Think of home, think of girls, think of anything but this pain!* Disappointed that Karl wasn't showing enough suffering, the guard let him go — after taking the rice for himself. It took weeks for the puncture wounds to heal.

Despite the punishment, Karl and Ike continued to steal food and help sabotage enemy supplies. While Karl acted as a lookout, Ike would pour water on the rice bags so they would rot in the summer heat before reaching their destination.

For four months, beginning in May 1945, American forces flew daily bombing runs over Tokyo and Yokohama — a sign that Japan was losing the war. The day the POWs — and all the free world — yearned for finally came on August 15. That morning, Karl and the others stepped outside and were surprised not to see any guards. Eventually, a guard showed up and said simply, "Your work is finished."

The bloodiest war in the history of mankind was over. So were Karl's three years of torment as a slave laborer.

When the plane carrying him home took off from Tokyo on September 2, Karl looked out the window and beamed at the sight below. There, anchored in Tokyo Bay, was the battleship USS *Missouri* where at that moment the Japanese were formally signing their surrender.

Karl sat back in his seat, never having felt so good. Despite being a teenage POW, he was a marine who had found a way to fight back.

Surrendered, yes. Defeated, no!

Of the 23 ships the POWs were forced to build in the Mitsubishi Shipyards during their captivity, 18 needed to return from their maiden voyage for repairs and 4 others capsized or sank on their own from sabotage.

Karl, who received several medals including the Bronze Star and Purple Heart, was discharged from the marines in 1947. While raising a family, he became a broadcast journalist in the Dallas area and retired in 1970. He wrote a book about his war experiences called Alamo of the Pacific, *which supplied some of the material for this story. Karl died in 2005 and was buried at Dallas–Fort Worth National Cemetery with full military honors.*

THE RESISTER

LUCIE VANOSMAEL

Lucie Vanosmael grunted but didn't scream when her Nazi torturer rubbed out his lighted cigarette on her bare arm. Strapped to a chair, Lucie gritted her teeth.

"Tell me who you work for!" demanded the Gestapo officer.

"I'm just a schoolgirl," she insisted. "I don't work for anyone."

He slapped her. "If you think I'm tough on you, wait until Colonel Schwartz arrives. He knows how to make a brat like you talk."

Lucie, who had been kept in ice-cold water for hours and beaten repeatedly with a rubber hose for three days, slumped in her chair. To ignore the pain and agony, she closed her eyes and pictured how her life was before the German invasion.

As a single child in a loving household, Lucie displayed a zest for life and carried a reputation as a fearless tomboy. The spunky auburn-haired girl rode her bike all over Brussels, the capital city of Belgium, often stopping to play soccer with the boys or climb trees or even swing on a trapeze at a neighborhood park. Flashing a dimpled smile wherever she went, the freckle-faced teenager charmed her way into a free *frangipane* — a Belgian pastry — from the baker or a praline from the *chocolatier* in exchange for sweeping the front of their shops.

Her patriotism came from her father, Guillaume, a highly decorated Belgian soldier who lost an arm during combat in World War I. He impressed upon her the importance of duty and loyalty to the nation. "Good citizenship," he told her, "also means helping others, especially the weak and defenseless."

So when German forces roared into Belgium in May 1940 at the beginning of World War II, 14-year-old Lucie decided to join the Resistance — an underground network of Belgians outraged by the German occupation and the Nazis' brutal treatment of Jews.

Knowing the Resistance wouldn't accept girls her age, Lucie changed her birth certificate to make herself appear two years older. Meeting the leader of an underground group, she impressed him with her zeal. The leader, who went by the code name *Zero*, said, "If you're captured, the Gestapo will torture you and then kill you or send you to a work camp. Are you prepared for that risk?"

"They won't catch me," she boasted. "And if they do, they won't get anything out of me. I'd rather die than betray my country."

Zero admired her spirit and her ability to speak German, French, and English. He made her a member and gave her the code name *Lulu*. She continued to attend school while leading a cloak-and-dagger double life unknown to her closest friends and even her parents. She became one of 200,000 Belgian resisters who harassed the Nazis, sabotaged installations and supply lines, helped escaped prisoners and downed Allied airmen, and distributed banned publications.

In Lucie's group were forgers who produced fake identity cards, work papers, German permits, Nazi membership cards, and Belgian passports. Most of these official documents had to be issued on special paper that she helped steal.

Lucie delivered many of these forged papers to various safe houses — places where the Resistance hid escaping Allied servicemen and Jews wanted by the Nazis. Whenever she carried secret messages and documents, she tucked them in her underwear. Usually at checkpoints, the Germans let the cheery schoolgirl go through after examining her identity card.

But one day, a soldier stopped her in the street and began conducting a full body search. As he patted her down, Lucie had to think fast before he found the hidden documents. Noticing that several people had stopped to watch her get frisked, Lucie loudly protested in perfect German, "You should be ashamed of yourself! No gentleman would dare touch a schoolgirl like this!"

The gathering crowd of mostly older adults voiced their outrage until the soldier blushed and stepped away. "My apologies, *Fraülein*," he said, motioning for her to move on. Once she turned the corner, she leaned against a building and took several deep breaths of relief. The soldier's fingers had been only an inch away from discovering the concealed documents.

Sometimes Lucie acted as a spy. She carried a large straw purse cluttered with items including a tiny camera. She would sit on a bench opposite local Nazi headquarters and photograph, through a small hole in her purse, people who entered and left the building. Her photos provided evidence that certain Belgians were collaborators (citizens secretly working for the enemy).

On occasion, she teamed up with an 18-year-old resister whose code name was *Marcel*. She enjoyed these assignments because he was good-looking and funny. Acting like boyfriend and girlfriend, they would stroll in front of a German ammunition dump or supply depot while she snapped pictures from her spy camera.

During the winter in 1941, Marcel planned to meet a Belgian officer who claimed to have a list of collaborators. "I'm seeing him at the Lioncrest Art Gallery," Marcel told Lucie. "It should take only a few minutes. Why don't you wait for me at the Bonpapa Café, and we'll have dinner together."

"I'd like that very much," Lucie said dreamily. "My parents think I am tutoring classmates tonight at the library."

After Marcel entered the gallery, Lucie decided to wait outside rather than sit in the café alone. It was such a pretty evening with a light snow falling. But then she heard a scuffle and gunshots. Suddenly, Marcel crashed through the plate-glass window and onto the sidewalk as a soldier in the gallery fired a machine gun.

Bleeding from his head, arm, and leg, Marcel was lying on his back, shooting a pistol. Lucie immediately dragged him behind a parked car, took his gun, and shot the soldier. Two other men inside fired handguns. Seeing them crouch next to a gas heater, Lucie shot it, triggering a small explosion and fire.

She helped Marcel to his feet and half carried him to a nearby safe house where he was treated for three gunshot wounds and several lacerations.

"I was set up, Lulu," Marcel said. "The man claimed he was Charles Hecht, a former major in the Belgian army. He had dark brown hair combed back and greased with a broad gray streak down the middle."

"Like a skunk," she growled.

"Yes, and he walks with a limp, and he's missing the top half of the last two fingers on his right hand. By the way, where did you learn to shoot so well?"

"Papa taught me. We have a small house in the country that we use on the weekends. He lets me shoot at tin cans."

A few days later, Zero called a meeting in the basement of a candy store to discuss the traitor who had infiltrated their organization. When Lucie arrived and glanced at the other members, she gasped, "Papa? What are you doing here?"

"I should ask you that question."

They had been working for the same underground network for more than a year without knowing the other was a member, too. "You're too young," he told her. "It's much too dangerous." He turned and said to Zero, "She's only a child. You must let her go."

"But I can't," Zero said. "She's very useful to us. We need her."

"Papa, you always told me that I had a duty to my country," she said. "I hate the Nazis and what they are doing to Belgium and the Jews."

He gave in and hugged her, saying, "We won't tell your mother. She'll die from worry if she knew we both are in the Resistance."

As part of their work with the underground, father and daughter were involved in the Comète Line, a Belgian network that helped escaped prisoners of war and downed Allied airmen safely return to their bases. The men were given civilian clothes, fake identity papers, and escorted from one safe house to another as they traveled from Belgium through France and into Spain.

Whenever the Vanosmaels were at their country house, Lucie and her father were on call, ready to search for airmen who had bailed out of crippled planes. During one summer weekend, they learned that two Americans had parachuted into the woods nearby. "We need to find them before the Germans do," her father told her. "We'll split up. If you reach them first, bring them to the basement of Saint Anthony's church."

"Are we still using the same song?" she asked.

"Yes. The airmen should know what it means."

While walking in the forest, Lucie tried to signal the airmen by singing a popular tune from the 1938 movie *Sweethearts*: "Far ahead, where the blue shadows fall / I shall come to contentment and rest / And the toils of the day / Will be all charmed away / In my little gray home of the west."

Eventually from behind a thicket, she heard a male voice sing, "In my little gray home of the west."

"It's safe to come out," she said.

Two Americans in their flight jackets emerged from the brush. They were in good shape, although they were tired, hungry, and thirsty. She brought them food and civilian clothes. Dressed like villagers and carrying fishing gear, the Americans ambled to the church by following Lucie from a safe distance. They hid there for several days until she brought them forged documents for their return along the Comète Line.

During another weekend, Lucie was looking for a downed British pilot in the woods. When she started to cross a busy country road, she screamed in horror. Dangling from nooses tied to a large oak tree were three dead men. Each had been shot in the back of the head. She recognized two as resisters. The third man was wearing the uniform of a British pilot. The Gestapo had hanged them as a warning to citizens not to help the Resistance.

Early one morning, Lucie went to a safe house to deliver fake documents for a downed pilot who was still sleeping. Minutes after Lucie arrived, two German soldiers knocked at the door. "Stall them as long as you can," she whispered to the safe house's elderly owner, Mrs. Thiery.

Lucie raced into the bedroom, shook the soldier awake, and ordered him to climb out the window and onto the roof. He threw on a shirt over his underwear and jumped into the slippers of Mrs. Thiery's late husband. Lucie shoved the airmen's clothes in his arms, helped him out the window, and closed it.

She figured the soldiers would barge in and place their hands on the empty bed. If it felt warm, they would know someone had been sleeping there. Lucie whipped off her dress and dived under the covers.

The door burst open, and she cried out in mock surprise. "Auntie," she said to Mrs. Thiery, "why are the soldiers here?"

"They think we are hiding an American pilot."

"Oh, that's silly," Lucie said, watching the Germans search the closet and under the bed. Out of the corner of her eye, she saw a slipper fall in front of the window. It also caught the attention of the soldiers. Wrapping a blanket around her, she dashed to the window, opened it up, and shouted, "Oh, no! It's Walter! He did it again and jumped off the roof."

"Who is Walter?" the soldiers demanded.

"Our cat. Thank goodness he landed on his feet. See? That's him over there," she said, pointing to a tabby that happened to be in the alley across the way.

Satisfied, the soldiers left. Mrs. Thiery hugged Lucie and said, "My, you're a fast thinker." Then the two helped the airman back into the house.

By age 16, Lucie was taking on more dangerous missions

that required training with automatic weapons, hand grenades, and dynamite. Over the next year, she helped destroy bridges by planting explosives, and she cut railway communications by climbing telephone poles and snipping the wires.

She was also a part of a squad that ambushed Nazi troops. One evening, she boldly stopped a four-truck German convoy by standing in the middle of a country road, waving a lantern. Before the soldiers could react, a dozen resisters bombarded the trucks with hand grenades, killing all on board.

The more she saw of the Nazi brutality toward Belgian Jews and resisters, the more inflamed she became. That's why she volunteered for a mission designed to kill hundreds of soldiers. While pretending to wait for a train at the bustling station in the suburb of Schaerbeek, Lucie carried a suitcase stuffed with dynamite. She entered the car of a train and then exited on the other side, handing off the suitcase to a fellow resister. She did the same thing with another suitcase. Then, late at night, she slipped under the platform and helped set up the dynamite charges.

The following day, a German troop train arrived at the station. Within seconds, a massive blast blew up the building, derailed the train, destroyed 10 passenger cars, and killed more than 600 German soldiers.

In the spring of 1944, Lucie carried a backpack filled with hollowed-out textbooks that held important documents. She was to give them to a man in a black Citroën parked in an alley behind the Bonpapa Café. When she arrived, a man in large horn-rimmed glasses, a fedora, and a dark coat stepped out of the car. He held out his right hand, which was sheathed in a black leather glove, and asked, "Lulu?"

She nodded and shook his hand. To Lucie, there was something odd about the handshake, but she didn't know what.

Taking her backpack, he said, "Please, get in my car. I have something important to tell you in strictest confidence." The moment she slid into the backseat, it hit her: *He's missing the last two fingers of his right hand! Oh, my God, he's the traitor!* She whipped open the door, but two husky men barged in from opposite sides and stuck guns in her ribs.

The man took off his hat, revealing slicked-back brown hair with a gray streak down the middle. "We're going for a little ride," he told her.

"You're the skunk!" she shouted.

Just as she dreaded, Lucie was whisked to Saint-Gilles, the main prison of Brussels. The grim, large complex was crammed with victims of German oppression: men and women from the Resistance; hostages who were innocent friends and relatives of suspected resisters; political foes; and captured Allied servicemen waiting to be shipped to POW camps in Germany.

Shoved into a small, windowless, stone-lined cell, Lucie mustered all the willpower she could not to panic. Her heart was beating so fast that she felt dizzy. *Stay calm,* Lucie told herself. *They'll torture me, but I must stay strong and silent no matter what.*

Later that night, Lieutenant Goetzfried from the Gestapo visited her cell. The tall, handsome man with thick neatly combed blond hair tried to comfort her. "I'm sure you are scared," he said. "Just answer our questions about the Resistance, and then you can go home."

"I don't know what you're talking about," she said. "I'm just a girl trying to get through high school."

He smiled and patted her on the head. "My dear," he said sweetly, "you are such a pretty girl, you don't belong in a place like this. You belong with your family and friends. I want to make sure you return home safely. All I need from you is a little cooperation." He patted her cheek and left.

A few hours later, Goetzfried returned and politely asked that she reveal the names of resisters. When she claimed she didn't know any, he shook his head and said softly, "What a pity." After he left, two guards yanked her out of her cell and threw her into a shallow pool of waist-high ice-cold water. Within minutes, she was shivering, her teeth were chattering, and her legs lost all feeling.

"I beg of you, give me the name of your leader," Goetzfried implored. "Give me the name of the resisters in your group, and I'll let you out and bring you warm towels."

"I . . . I'm j . . . just a st . . . student tr . . . trying t . . . to g . . . get thr . . . through sch . . . school," she stammered.

"Sadly, I have run out of patience." Facing the guards, Goetzfried ordered, "Keep her in there for another hour. Make sure she doesn't drown. I want her to suffer."

In the frigid cold, Lucie lost consciousness and sank to the bottom. A guard pulled her out and carried her to her cell. But the next morning, the still wet and shaking girl was dragged back to the pool and tossed in again. Again, she refused to talk.

By the third day, Lucie was barely conscious. Suffering from hunger and hypothermia (loss of body heat), she couldn't speak even if she wanted to. In frustration, Goetzfried beat her with a hose until she passed out. The following day, she was given her first meal since she had been captured — cabbage soup and bread.

Then the questioning began again. Goetzfried threatened and beat her. But nothing he said or did — even burning her arms with lighted cigarettes — could pry any information out of the gutsy teenager.

Giving up, he called in Colonel Schwartz, an overweight, beady-eyed man with a permanent scowl. When he couldn't wring out any useful information from Lucie, he ordered the guards, "Take her out in the yard and tie her to the stake." He hissed at Lucie, "Prepare yourself, *Fraulein*, for I am about to execute you."

Weary from lack of sleep and food and numb from torture, she all but welcomed the thought of dying. *At least it will end my suffering.*

Minutes later, Lucie's arms were tied to a tall, bloodstained wooden post. Schwartz strode up to her, pulled out his pistol, cocked it, and pressed it against her forehead. "Tell me the names of the leaders of the Resistance, and I will spare your life," he said. "Otherwise, you die."

"I don't know who they are," she lied. "Do you think I would go through all this torture if I knew? I'm just a high school student."

He cursed her, lowered the gun, and stormed off.

Lucie was thrown back into her cell. *I'm still alive.* She didn't know how much more psychological and physical abuse she could take. Still, she would rather die than give up a single name, and so she prepared herself for death.

The next day, she was tied to the same post again. Colonel Schwartz marched up to her and put his weapon against her temple. "I must have the names, or this time I will kill you."

"I cannot give you what I don't have." She closed her eyes and waited for the fatal bullet to pierce her brain. It didn't happen. For the second time, Schwartz didn't follow through on his threat and stormed off in anger.

The torture continued; her body was covered in cigarette burns and welts. But still, she wouldn't talk. Later that day, Lucie was hauled out once more to the post.

Colonel Schwartz whispered in her ear, "My superiors think I'm weak because I haven't executed you. I have no choice now. Either you reveal the names of your leaders this instant, or I absolutely will kill you. You have five seconds."

Oh, God, this is it, she thought.

"Five . . ."

Poor Mommy and Daddy.

"Four . . ."

I didn't rat out the leaders.

"Three . . ."

My death is for a just cause.

"Two . . ."

I hate the Nazis.

"One . . ."

Lucie closed her eyes. And, believing she had only a single second of life left, she chose as her last words, "Freedom for Belgium!"

Bang! Bang! Bang! Lucie waited for the pain, for the silence, for the curtain of death to descend upon her. But there was none of that. She still breathed. She still felt the rope around her wrists and the post pressing on her back. She opened her eyes. *I'm not dead.*

Colonel Schwartz stared at her. Lucie could detect a slight smile hiding behind his scowl. It was now obvious that he had fired the three shots into a barrel a few feet behind the post.

"If you truly are nothing more than a schoolgirl, then you don't deserve to die," he told her. "On the other hand, I still believe you are hiding the truth from me. If so, I admire your iron will. It is stronger than many of my own soldiers." He untied her. "I will spare your life, *Fraülein*. But I'm not convinced you are as innocent as you claim, so I am sending you to a labor camp."

I'm not dead.

Within a week, Lucie had been transferred to a slave camp in Germany where she was forced to work in a munitions factory, making parts for bombs. As was the same for all the forced laborers, if she didn't assemble each device correctly, she was beaten or had food taken away.

One evening, at the end of a shift, she spotted a woman's full-length coat and hat lying on a bench outside the door to the factory office. Without hesitation, she put them on over her prison garb and walked out. She made it past the first checkpoint when a guard about 10 yards behind her ordered her to stop and show her papers. *It's now or never,* she thought. Lucie made a zigzagging dash for freedom down the street while the guard shot at her. Just as she was ducking into an alley, Lucie was struck in the arm. She lost her balance, falling to the pavement and smacking her head hard enough to knock her out.

She wound up in a hospital ward under an armed guard. "We were warned that you were a strong-minded girl," said an officer. "That's a good trait to have. But here it can get you killed. If you try to escape again, we will shoot you dead."

Lucie had been threatened so many times before that she paid little attention to this one. A few months later, while she was in an open-air transport truck full of workers, she noticed the two guards with them had their backs turned on her. She leaped off the truck, tumbled on the dirt road, rolled into the shoulder, and then hid in the weeds. As she had hoped, none of the other prisoners said a word.

Over the next six weeks, the plucky girl walked more than 100 miles, moving only in darkness, to the home of fellow resisters in Holland. She lived on raw eggs and vegetables that she stole from farms along the way and slept in haystacks and barns during the day. Every step took greater effort than the one before because she was weak, sick, and hungry. But nothing could stop her from returning home. By the time she reached the Dutch resisters, she was feverish and malnourished. Her hair and teeth were falling out.

Lucie eventually made it home and regained her health. Despite all she had gone through, she continued her work as a resister until that glorious September day in 1944 when British forces liberated Brussels. Men, women, and children cheered and wept for joy. They tossed flowers to the troops and sprayed them with champagne.

Crying and laughing at the same time, Lucie leaped onto a British army tank that had strayed from the convoy. The operator poked his head out of the hatch and said, "Hey, miss, I think I'm lost. Where am I?"

"Where are you?" Lucie giggled. "Why, this is heaven!"

After the war, Lucie, who received several honors for her resistance efforts, worked as a volunteer to help Belgian POWs return to their homes and jobs. In 1946, she married a British naval officer and moved to England. After becoming a widow, she married Englishman David Bruce in 1976. She had three children, two stepchildren, five grandchildren, and three great-grandchildren. She died in England in 2007. Said her husband at her funeral, "Lucie had a remarkable life and was incredibly brave in the face of the Nazis. Her hatred for them never mellowed. She was opposed to them until the end. Compared with most of us, she had lived a thousand lives by the time she was twenty."

THE TEENAGE WAR VET

JAMES E. (JIM) WARD

Fourteen-year-old Jim Ward was already six feet tall, too big to play with kids his own age and too young to hang around people his own size. He hated school and loved to fight.

Bored with class, the Greensboro, North Carolina, teenager quit school after seventh grade. But he was smart enough to understand that if he wanted to stay out of trouble, he'd better join the army. And he knew just how to do it.

First, he convinced his mother. He explained that it was in his best interests to enlist "so they can make a man out of me." Because money was tight for the family of seven, enlisting would ease the financial burden, he told her, and mean one less mouth to feed, one less body to clothe. Then he appealed to her patriotism, and that secured her approval.

What Jim didn't want to do was face his father, George, who was angry the teenager had quit school. Even so, Jim hoped his dad would understand. The boy was only trying to follow in the footsteps of his father who had joined the army illegally at age 15 and fought in World War I.

George became a teenage hero by single-handedly destroying five machine-gun nests and capturing 17 enemy troops during a German assault in 1918 in France. In fierce hand-to-hand combat, a German soldier speared him with a bayonet all the way through his left leg. The wound became severely infected, and his limb was amputated. Earning the Distinguished Service Cross, George, who also suffered from shrapnel wounds, returned home to work in a foundry and raise a family.

Jim felt it was his turn now to enlist as an underage soldier. He put on his older brother Tom's good suit and carefully groomed his hair the way adults did back then to hide his youth. It was 1949, a time when the military had downsized following the end of World War II. Although trouble was brewing in Asia, America was at peace.

He walked into the recruiting office and claimed he was 17 — the minimum age to enlist with parental consent. Explaining why he had only his mother's written approval, Jim lied, saying, "My parents are separated, and I haven't seen my dad in a year." The recruiter signed him up, and Jim headed to Fort Jackson, South Carolina, for basic training. He left it up to his mother to tell his father.

Throughout boot camp, Jim showed he was every bit as

good a trainee as the others, even though he was at least three years younger than the rest. He became skilled at marching, shooting at targets, cleaning weapons, throwing grenades, and guard duty. During his first leave, Jim returned home where he finally faced his father. Whatever worries Jim had melted away when George gave his blessing.

Jim then was sent to Fort Lewis, Washington, for advanced combat training. Being so far away from home, the 14-year-old grew increasingly homesick. He missed his family and wanted to give up and go home, so he requested a meeting with the camp commander.

"Colonel," said Jim. "I want to get out of the army."

The colonel, a kind and fatherly figure, seemed surprised. "You have the makings of becoming a fine soldier, son. Why in the world do you want to quit?"

"I miss my home and my family."

"We all do, son. You'll have to do better than that."

"Okay." Jim lowered his eyes and revealed, "I'm only fourteen years old."

The news nearly floored the colonel, who pressed Jim for the details of how such a young boy fooled the army. After hearing Jim's story, the colonel said, "Private Ward, despite your age, I'm convinced that kicking you out of the military would do you more harm than good. You won't return to school. You'll just get in trouble. Why don't you stay in the army and become a man? I'll even arrange for you to attend night school on the base."

"But won't you get in trouble for keeping me here?"

The colonel winked and replied, "I won't say anything if you won't."

After his training, Jim was shipped to South Korea in July 1950, which had just been invaded by the communist North Koreans. His unit joined a relatively small American force under the U.N. command. The soldiers' job was to hold off the better-equipped and more experienced invaders until the U.S. military could build up its strength and launch a counteroffensive.

While the enemy streamed across the South Korean border using powerful Soviet-built tanks and heavy artillery, the Americans had weapons that were castoffs from World War II. Some of the rifles didn't work or were damaged from previous combat. Because mortar ammunition was old, more than half the rounds failed to explode. Few radios worked.

When his unit — the Twenty-ninth Regimental Combat Team — arrived in Korea, Jim was greeted by furnace-hot temperatures and flies so thick they sometimes flew into his mouth when he tried to speak or eat. Because of the lack of drinking water, the men filled their canteens from rice paddies, not realizing these ponds were contaminated by human and animal waste. Galloping diarrhea struck nearly every soldier.

Jim and 700 comrades were ordered toward the town of Hadong because intelligence indicated a band of enemy guerrillas was roaming in the hills. Like virtually all the green troops, Jim had never fired his weapon in combat and didn't know what to expect. His superiors played down any concerns, saying the mission would be easy and would give them "good field experience."

On the night of July 24, a mile from Hadong, Jim joined a patrol that searched for the guerrillas. After walking a half mile, he spotted a massive number of tiny, twinkling red lights along the slopes of the nearby mountains.

"What are they?" he asked his patrol leader, Sergeant Dave Hartigan.

"I don't know. Maybe lightning bugs?"

Jim shook his head. "They remind me of something familiar from back home, but I can't quite put my finger on it."

Not seeing signs of the enemy, the patrol headed back and soon encountered a wagonload of wounded South Korean citizens fleeing from Hadong. In broken English, they told the Americans that the North Korean army was camped on the mountains.

"How many?" asked Jim.

"Thousands and thousands," came the reply.

"Oh, geez," Jim told Hartigan. "I know what those glowing red lights are — and they sure aren't lightning bugs. I used to see them when I went hunting with my uncles at night. They're lit cigarettes!"

Back at the command post, the officers refused to believe there were so many enemy soldiers that close and ordered the men to move into Hadong at daybreak. The next morning, the soldiers entered a valley bordered on three sides by the same mountains where Jim saw the lights. Without warning, machine-gun fire, mortars, and artillery poured into the valley. The ground shook and the slopes echoed from the deafening blasts.

Terrified beyond belief, Jim didn't know what to do or where to run for cover. To him, the enemy was firing from every direction. "What's happening?" he shouted to no one in particular.

"We're caught in an ambush!" Hartigan yelled.

What he wouldn't learn until later was that the 700 U.S. greenhorns had just stepped into a killing field surrounded by 12,000 hardened soldiers from the Sixth North Korean Division. The rookie Americans didn't stand a chance. They were outgunned, outmanned, and outflanked.

Wherever Jim looked, men were falling. *My God,* he thought, *it's like shooting fish in a barrel.* He hopped onto a Jeep that spun 180 degrees and started to roar back, joining a fleeing convoy. But the enemy had sealed off the escape route. When Jim saw the first vehicle in the convoy blow up from a direct hit, he and the others leaped off their jeeps and found whatever cover they could. Crouching behind a rock, he turned around just in time to see the jeep he had been riding in explode and erupt in flames.

Fighting panic, Jim had yet to fire his weapon. He wasn't sure where to shoot because he hadn't seen the face of a single North Korean. No training had prepared him for this — a massacre in his first combat experience. It wasn't anything like the war movies he had watched back home. The screen couldn't possibly portray the terror he was feeling, the horror he was witnessing, or the din he was hearing. In the movies, guns never jammed, ammo never ran out, soldiers never acted confused — all of which was happening at this moment.

Jim began firing into the foothills closest to him where enemy muzzles flashed. He shot with a vengeance, blindly and frantically. While reloading, he glanced to his left and right. His stomach churned at the sight of bodies sprawled every which way. *It's a slaughter out here,* he thought. *Will I ever get out of this alive?*

He blasted away until he ran out of ammo, so he crawled over to several dead comrades, took their bullets and continued shooting. The North Koreans were now emerging from their positions and swarming into the valley. *They'll kill us all!*

"Fall back!" Hartigan shouted. Jim leaped to his feet and joined a few dozen soldiers as they sprinted toward a spot in the rear that the enemy had failed to close off. Jim's survival instincts told him to keep fleeing, but he couldn't — not when the wounded lay on the ground. "We can't leave them behind!" he shouted to the others.

They turned around and hurriedly helped carry off the wounded closest to them and then slipped into the thick foliage. "We need to split up into small groups of five or six so the enemy will have a harder time finding us," Hartigan said. "Find your own way back to our lines."

"But isn't that about forty miles from here?" Jim asked.

Hartigan glared at him. "It is what it is. Now go!"

Fearing a pursuit by the enemy, Jim and his group hustled as best they could with their wounded comrades. The going became so rigorous that some threw away their machine guns, ammunition, rifles, and helmets. Despite his young age, Jim kept pace into the night and next day. They scrambled over steep hills, crossed streams up to 20 feet deep, and slogged through smelly rice paddies until they reached friendly lines.

More than 300 Americans were killed in that ambush and another 100 were captured. Because of the massive losses, Jim, like most of the survivors, was reassigned to the Twenty-seventh Regiment of the Twenty-fifth Division and put at a different front, this time defending the perimeter near the South Korean city of Pusan. "If you weren't ready for combat near Hadong, you sure are now," Hartigan told him.

"The brass have issued a 'stand or die' order," the sergeant told his men. "We must hold this line for at least six weeks until reinforcements arrive. No more retreating. We must gut it out. We must win."

Jim, now a corporal, was assigned to a foxhole at a key point on the perimeter. For the next three weeks, he and his comrades fought off repeated enemy attacks. North Korean squads poured over the hills and through the gaps like a flood, but Jim and his fellow Americans refused to give in. The daily fighting had quickly turned him into a seasoned soldier — and a wet, tired, and bewildered one. He had been swept from the peaceful United States and been tossed into the middle of an ugly war against a vicious enemy in a divided country.

The ground was littered with the dead — more enemy soldiers than Americans. One time during a fierce firefight, Jim was caught in the open. The only way to save himself was to stack a few dead soldiers in front of him and use them as cover until he worked his way to a safer area.

Another time, when Jim was at a hilltop outpost, he saw in the distance an entire American platoon surrender. The North Koreans marched the POWs out to a point beyond Jim's rifle range but still within eyesight. Through binoculars, he saw the enemy tie the captives' hands behind their backs — and then shoot them in the head.

Jim shook from rage and revulsion. He told Hartigan, "I'll never be taken alive by these butchers."

Later Jim felt another wave of fury, but this time coupled with nausea, when his platoon moved through the area where he had witnessed the execution. He turned his eyes away as his unit marched somberly past the ditch where the slain Americans lay.

That night, Jim dug his foxhole even deeper, filled his army belt with extra grenades, and strapped another bandolier of bullets across his chest.

The scariest time for Jim was at dusk, when the shadows grew long and he could see the North Koreans crawling around like ants, positioning for another attack. The enemy used bugles, whistles, and gongs to communicate with one another — and to unnerve the Americans during regular nighttime attacks that seemed to last forever.

On the morning of September 15, 1950, artillery and mortar fire began to fall on Jim's position. After one shell exploded only a few yards away, he was nearly buried by debris. Shaking off the rocks and dirt, he became aware of a sharp, burning pain in his forearm. He gasped when he saw he had been struck by a smoldering piece of jagged metal. He closed his eyes, gritted his teeth, and yanked the shrapnel out. *I'll worry about this later.*

He had more pressing problems. Swarms of enemy soldiers fanned out in a wide movement, sweeping in from the east and west up the far slopes of the hill that he and his unit were defending.

"Follow me!" ordered Hartigan. They dashed toward another position when the sergeant spun around and faced Jim. Blood from a massive bullet wound gushed from Hartigan's forehead. He stared at Jim with a blank, frozen look and then fell dead at Jim's feet.

The teenager couldn't mourn. He had to act fast. Turning to the rest of the shocked squad, he ordered, "Keep moving to that rock! Double-time!" Once they gathered, he took over the sergeant's role. Pointing to three soldiers on his left, he told them, "Go about fifty feet to your left and keep tossing grenades." Addressing the three comrades who had machine guns, he ordered, "Set up over here and aim at that cluster of rocks. The Koreans have to pass through that spot if they plan on rushing us."

Without any hesitation, Jim continued to direct his men. His quick thinking and clear orders stopped the enemy from advancing on the squad. "It's our turn now!" he told his fellow soldiers. "Attack!" With the men following his every order, Jim led a charge that quickly routed the North Koreans.

When his squad returned to the rear lines, his commanding officer told Jim, "Ward, I heard what you did out there today. I'm putting in a recommendation for you for the Silver Star."

"Thank you, sir!" For a brief moment, the praise and good news had blotted out the sadness he felt over Hartigan's death.

"You've shown you're a damn good soldier, Sergeant."

Pointing to the emblem on his sleeve, Jim said, "Begging your pardon, sir, but I'm a corporal."

"Not anymore," said the officer, handing him his sergeant's stripes.

The teenage sergeant was now in charge of a squad of men who were much older, including a few twice his age. He tried to look older by growing a mustache and lowering his voice when he talked. But that was for appearance's sake. When it mattered most, during the heat of combat, he made snap decisions worthy of a veteran soldier.

Still, there were nights that scared him to death — fighting a fanatical enemy that screeched like banshees whenever they attacked. Even worse were the times when he had a split second to decide whether he was shooting at a North Korean soldier or an innocent South Korean citizen. In one of their sneakiest tricks, the enemy infiltrators dressed up like elderly Korean women and, posing as refugees moving south from the fighting, walked past the Americans' outposts. Then they whipped out their hidden weapons, turned around, and attacked the soldiers from behind.

One day, after returning from a patrol on the front line, Jim was ordered to see the commanding officer. This time the officer wasn't smiling. He said, "Sergeant Ward, your mother wants you."

"I don't understand, sir."

"Tell me something, Sergeant. Just how old are you *really*?"

Jim's heart sank. *Uh-oh. They're on to me.* "I'm sixteen, sir."

"My God, how old were you when you enlisted?"

"Fourteen, sir."

"Well, you were too young then, and you're too young now to serve. We're sending you home."

"But you promoted me and said I was a good soldier," Jim argued.

"Yeah, you're a good soldier who lied to get into the army. I can't have a *child* in my unit."

"How did you find out?"

"Your older brother, Tom, had volunteered for the army's Ranger program and is heading to Korea. Your father didn't want to have two sons in combat at the same time, so he wrote to [General Douglas] MacArthur, telling him you're too young to be fighting. Your father enclosed a copy of your birth certificate and added that your mother is worried sick about you."

Jim had mixed emotions. He felt an obligation to his comrades and country to fight, but he was more than ready to leave this dreadful war behind. The army sent him to San Francisco where he had a brief reunion with Tom.

Before taking the train home to North Carolina, Jim spent a day with a photographer for *Life* magazine. The following month, the magazine published a photo of Jim in uniform leaving the building where he had been mustered out. With a duffel bag perched on his shoulder, Jim was sporting a wispy mustache. Over his heart were pinned several medals, including a combat infantry badge and the Purple Heart. The headline that accompanied the photo summed up his military life: AN OLD SOLDIER RETIRES AT 16.

Jim never saw combat again. Upon his return home to Greensboro, North Carolina, he worked at a Sears store rather than go back to school. (He later admitted to a local newspaper that not completing his high school education "was the biggest mistake I ever made.") After turning 17, he reenlisted and spent three more years in the service. Back in Greensboro, he married, raised a family, and made his living working in a foundry.

ABOUT THE AUTHOR

Allan Zullo is the author of more than 90 nonfiction books on subjects ranging from sports and the supernatural to history and animals.

He has written the bestselling *Haunted Kids* series, published by Scholastic, which are filled with chilling stories based on, or inspired by, documented cases from the files of ghost hunters. Allan also has introduced Scholastic readers to the *Ten True Tales* series, gripping stories of extraordinary persons — many of them young people — who have met the challenges of dangerous, sometimes life-threatening, situations. One of the books in the series is *World War II Heroes.* In addition, he has authored two books about the real-life experiences of kids during the Holocaust — *Survivors: True Stories of Children in the Holocaust* and *Heroes of the Holocaust: True Stories of Rescues by Teens.*

Allan, the grandfather of three boys and the father of two grown daughters, lives with his wife, Kathryn, on a mountainside near Asheville, North Carolina. To learn more about the author, visit his Web site at www.allanzullo.com.